Classic Resorts
&
Romantic Retreats

A Guide for the Discriminating Traveler

Written by Lewis Green
Photographed by Kay Green

New Horizons Publishers
Seattle

Published by New Horizons Publishers
P.O. Box 20744
Seattle, WA 98102

Library of Congress Catalog Number:
85-63458

ISBN: 0-915325-02-0

Typesetting: Magna Color Press, Inc.
Seattle, Washington

Printed by Toppan Printing Co., Ltd.
Tokyo, Japan

Design and Production:
Kay Green

Penthouse Suite, The Sorrento Hotel, Seattle, Washington

Lewis Green is a travel writer living in Seattle. When he's not on the road, he can usually be found sitting at his typewriter. His work regularly appears in newspapers and magazines, including The Los Angeles Times, The Portland Oregonian, Washington Magazine and Oregon Magazine. In addition, Lewis often guests on regional radio and television talk shows. This is his third travel guidebook. Kay Green is a photographer whose work has appeared in such publications as The Los Angeles Times and The Portland Oregonian. This is also her third book.

Lewis and Kay Green's last book, **Fairs & Festivals of the Pacific Northwest**, is the only complete guide to fairs and festivals in Oregon, Washington and British Columbia. For a copy send a check in the amount of $5.50 to:

Fairs & Festivals of the Pacific Northwest
New Horizons Publishers
P.O. Box 20744
Seattle, WA 98102

Sunroom, The Beaconsfield Inn, Victoria, British Columbia

CONTENTS

Traveling In Style

I grew up in New Hampshire. When I look back, my mind fills with thoughts of the ocean washing across sandy beaches and exploding against rocky bluffs. I see mountains rising above forests thick with life and valleys spawning pristine lakes and colorful wildflowers.

Then, in 1964, I waved good-bye to New England's charms and spent the next 19 years searching for the promised land. My travels landed me and my wife, Kay, in Seattle three years ago. I felt as if I had met an old friend. Like New England, this landscape touches the very essence of humanity, but the dimensions here stretch the imagination. The ocean is deeper, the mountains higher, the valleys wider and the cities livelier.

Immediately upon arriving, Kay and I began having an affair with the West Coast. We wanted to experience all of it, to see its beauty and to taste its fruits. So Kay, armed with camera, and I, armed with pen, set out on a journey of discovery.

Although we have been known to enjoy the freedom of camping on a mountainside, Kay and I prefer the good life when we're on the road – what I call "traveling in style." Brass beds, country pine antiques, marbled baths, gourmet food and 24-hour room service make up things we take very seriously.

The Heathman Hotel

Four Seasons Olympic

Therefore, when we started out on this expedition, we had very specific objectives in mind. Not only did we want to walk on the beaches, hike through the mountains and play in the cities, we also wanted to be pampered. Our mission, as we saw it, was to find the best places in a region bursting with great getaways. At first it seemed as if we were on a mission impossible. But we persevered.

Since 1983 we have hung our clothes bags in more than 250 hotels, resorts and inns from San Francisco, California, to Gold Bridge, British Columbia. Our bodies have reclined on brass beds, tester beds, high antique beds and plain old bed-beds. We have bathed in surroundings of marble, chrome and polished wood. We have savored this area's freshest seafood, beef and poultry. And we have tested the skills and patience of waiters, housekeepers, valets, innkeepers and desk clerks. Through it all, we managed to write two guidebooks and a series of magazine articles reflecting some of our experiences and findings.

Now, however, we present the ultimate report on our travels. "Classic Resorts & Romantic Retreats" features both the best of the best and the best of the rest. From our journey we have selected what we believe to be the 52 finest hotels, resorts and inns in Oregon, Washington and British Columbia. And in case there's no room at the inn, we offer 29 alternative getaways for this region. In addition, we provide a special section on Northern California, which lists 15 first-class hostelries in an area covering San Francisco, the wine country, Marin County and the north coast.

Naturally, our choices represent our passions. No guidebook such as this can claim otherwise. Nevertheless, in making our selections we solicited the opinions of dozens of hoteliers, innkeepers, general managers, travel writers, restaurant reviewers, magazine editors and frequent travelers. We also established guidelines by which to judge a place's quality.

Location stood atop our list. Vacationers seldom travel to a getaway because of what it alone offers. Beyond a pleasant ambiance and good food, we want to be entertained. That may mean whiling away the hours eyeing the scenery or shopping a city's chiquest boutiques, but it seldom translates into traveling to the middle of Nowhere, unless Nowhere conjures up images of Utopia. So, to begin with, we sought establishments with prime locations.

Once there, we looked for first-class service. At first, cosmetic impressions often excite travelers: Grand architecture, rich woods, marble trim and expensive antiques inevitably implant their marks. However, these decorous items strike fleeting impacts. When guests check out, they evaluate their stays as either good, bad or indifferent based primarily on how well they were treated. Was the staff friendly, helpful, knowledgeable, professional and efficient? Did they care about special needs? What extras were provided to make the stay more comfortable? In every instance, the places featured in "Classic Resorts & Romantic Retreats" offer good to excellent service.

Alexis (Portland)

Next we judged the quality of the food. Besides shopping, eating ranks as one of North America's favorite pastimes. Unlike some, who believe quantity deserves special notice, we concerned ourselves with quality. Was the food seasonally fresh? Did the breads and pastries smell and taste homemade? Was a leisurely pace encouraged, or did the waiter just want to get on to his next tip? Was the wine list carefully designed or merely haphazardly thrown together? And, most important, was the preparation of the food of the highest quality?

As you might expect, we discovered most of the food to be average to good. In some instances, we found exceptionally exciting cuisine, but those were rare delights.

Our checklist also included decor, ambiance and comfort. Although anyone can purchase a brass bed and place it in a guest room, a certain talent and caring attitude are required in order for interior design to create a favorable impact. Naturally, we looked for things such as tasteful color schemes, rich fabrics and wall coverings, plush carpets or hardwood floors, private and roomy bathrooms, ample space in closets, comfortable furnishings, large windows and warm coverings. In public rooms, one criteria above all others most influenced our evaluation: Did we feel welcome and enjoy lingering, or did the surroundings make us want to retreat to our room?

Designer toiletries seem to be all the rage these days. Why not? I think perfumed soap and individually wrapped shower caps reflect caring attitudes. In fact, amenities played substantial roles in helping us make our final selections. Fireplaces, wet bars, terry robes, thick towels, saunas, whirlpools, swimming pools, tennis courts and golf courses, as well as custom toiletries, all contribute to the enjoyment of guests.

The places described on the following pages meet these standards. However, we also wanted to provide you with variety and choice, so we fit the criteria to the hostelry rather than making the hostelry squeeze into our slots. In other words, we judged based upon the perceived objectives of the lodging. We didn't expect a lodge such as Little Gun Lake or a resort such as Yellow Point, which boast relaxation in remote surroundings, to offer the kinds of amenities that can be expected of a Four Seasons Hotel in Seattle. Instead, we evaluated each place knowing that every traveler has individual needs and seeks different surroundings. However, we always kept in mind that all guests expect quality and value, whether they're going to the back woods or to cosmopolitan Vancouver.

Traveling in style means different things to different people. No place exists that suits every person. Knowing the risks that a book such as this takes, we offer you what we believe to be this region's best.

Wedgewood

Oregon

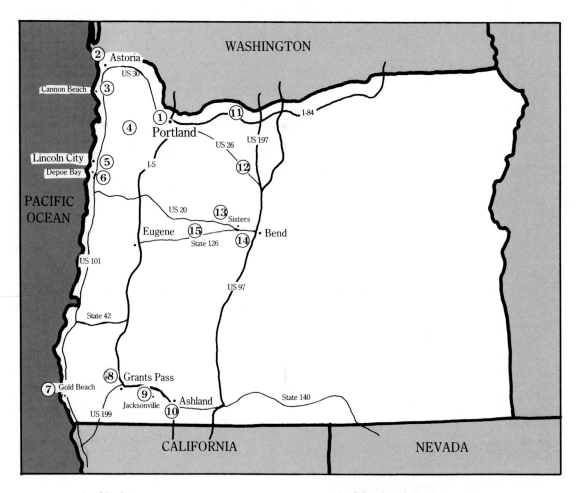

1. Alexis
   The Heathman Hotel
   The Westin Benson
2. Rosebriar Inn
3. New Surfview Resort
4. Flying M Ranch
5. Salishan Lodge
6. Channel House
7. Tu Tú Tun Lodge

8. Morrison's Lodge
9. Jacksonville Inn
10. Chanticleer Bed & Breakfast Inn
11. Columbia Gorge Hotel
12. Rippling River Resort
13. Black Butte Ranch
14. Inn of the Seventh Mountain
15. The Wayfarer Resort

For more information about Oregon, write or call:

**Economic Development Department
Tourism Division
595 Cottage Street N.E.
Salem, OR 97310
(800) 233-3306 (Inside Oregon)
(800) 547-7842 (Outside Oregon)**

Oceanside, Oregon

Mt. Bachelor, Oregon

Columbia River with Mt. Hood in the background

Marten Creek, Vida, Oregon

Chanticleer Bed & Breakfast Inn

"There is nothing which has yet been contrived by man by which so much happiness is produced as by a good tavern or inn." While Boswell's maxim sprouts gray hair, its message still holds truth for today's travelers.

For people on the road, a good inn sparkles like a polished gem. Chanticleer's glitter has been attracting happy guests since July of 1981. As testimony to its pleasures, the December 1984 issue of "Oregon Magazine" rated Chanticleer Oregon's best bed-and-breakfast inn.

The gray clapboard bungalow resides on a quiet residential tree-lined street just minutes from downtown Ashland. A terra-cotta brick walkway winds to the stone porch, while manicured lawns and a laurel hedge dress the yard. In the distance, the Cascade foothills form a rolling backdrop.

Warm summer breezes and golden sunlight splash across the home's spacious living room. Shelves of books sidle alongside the stone fireplace. Stuffed furniture surrounds a large oak coffee table, and four ladderback chairs encircle a hand-painted table depicting the four seasons.

Each of the seven guest rooms emanates an individual charm and personality. They range in size from the cozy main floor "Maître," with an antique brass bed and French window, to the downstairs two-bedroom "Chanticleer Suite," featuring a vaulted ceiling and a private yard. Antiques and comforters garnish every room. In addition, each accommodation includes a private bath and air conditioning.

Nevertheless, decor and charm do not define an outstanding inn. Behind every great guest house stand personable and tireless innkeepers. At Chanticleer, Jim and Nancy Beaver make every visitor feel welcome and special. Guests are coddled and cared for from the moment they arrive until the time they leave.

The Beavers' pampering includes extras such as complimentary beverages awaiting in the help-yourself kitchen, personal recommendations for dining or sightseeing, special year-round packages, fresh flowers garnishing each room, turned-down beds and tiny mints greeting retiring guests and gourmet breakfasts featuring homemade fare. All services are performed with smiles and grace.

While it may be tempting to while away the hours here, don't! Ashland boasts one of the area's richest tourist communities. From February to October, the world-famous Oregon Shakespearean Festival (482-4331) dons its dramatic masks; the Rogue Valley Symphony (482-6353) performs from October through May; Lithia Park contains 100 acres of magnificent parkland; and the town abounds with museums and galleries.

It is no wonder that this village of 15,000 attracts several hundred thousand visitors each year. Chanticleer is an inn that many of them now call their home away from home.

Travel Notes and Insider Tips

Gresham Street exits East Main Street just before the Ashland Public Library. The inn is located on the left-hand side.

Summer reservations for Chanticleer should be made several months in advance. Stop by the Ashland Chamber of Commerce (110 East Main) to pick up some very helpful brochures. Contact the Shakespearean Festival for a schedule of events. Don't miss Lithia Park or the Hanson Howard Galleries (488-2562). The Winchester Inn (488-1115) is renowned for its fine dining and ambiance, but if you want a taste of local flavor amidst natural Italian cuisine visit Geppetto's (482-1138).

Chanticleer's double rates range from $64 to $89 – breakfast is included. All prices are subject to change and are provided only for comparison.

Chanticleer Bed & Breakfast Inn
120 Gresham Street
Ashland, OR 97520
(503) 482-1919

Jacksonville Inn

The tiny Old West mining town of Jacksonville exemplifies the tenacious spirit of our earliest pioneer days. Born in 1851, fledgling Jacksonville received regular visits from tragedy. By 1860 its lifeblood, gold, had been mined out; just eight years later small pox swept through the dwindling community; in 1869 mud and rock wreaked havoc on the town's center; and then a few years later fire leveled most of the village's frame buildings.

Nevertheless, Jacksonville prevailed. Today thousands of travelers visit this National Historic Landmark. Its earlier brick structures look much the same as they did more than a century ago and dozens of historic buildings have been restored.

One such place is the Jacksonville Inn. The two-story brick building dates back to 1863. Like its host community, the inn is a survivor, and its owners, Jerry and Linda Evans, embody the community's spunky spirit.

Jerry and Linda purchased the inn in 1976 both to fulfill a lifelong dream and to avoid a corporate move away from their home in the Rogue River Valley. The restaurant was Jerry's first love and ultimately the key to the inn's success.

"There's a lot of phony things done in the restaurant business," Jerry explains. "We're just not into all the pomp and circumstance. We're into good food."

And good food is exactly what guests discover here. In fact, "Oregon Magazine" rated the Jacksonville Inn one of the state's ten best restaurants of 1985. In addition, restaurant critic Gloria Bledsoe, renowned for her no-nonsense reviews, wrote in a 1982 "diner's choice" column: "The atmosphere is marvelous . . . . The service is perfect . . . . some of the best food in Oregon."

Entrees, ranging from veal piccata, to New York pepper steak, to Australian lobster tail, may be ordered a la carte or as part of a full seven-course meal. As well as excellent food, the restaurant features a wine list of some 600 select choices.

The restaurant sits in the inn's lower level amongst sandstone walls still speckled with gold dust, massive fir beams, marbled mirrors, a gas brick fireplace, photographs of historic Jacksonville, red tablecloths and fresh flowers. It is dimly lit and refreshingly cool.

Each of the eight upstairs guest rooms also emanates charm: brass fixtures, oak headboards, antique chairs, floral print wallpaper and brick outer walls. Private bathrooms and air conditioning are standard fare.

The Jacksonville Inn is country – it is the Northwest. Visitors to southern Oregon should discover the ambiance and the fare for themselves.

Travel Notes and Insider Tips

Jacksonville sits about 275 miles south of Portland and 15 miles north of Ashland. Exit 238 off I-5 and drive seven miles west to Jacksonville.

One of the best but busiest times to visit is from June to August during Peter Britt Festivals (773-6077). The program series features jazz, bluegrass and country, and classical music, as well as a dance program. White-water rafting down the Rogue River and downhill skiing at Mt. Ashland are only a short drive away. Be sure to stop at the Jacksonville Chamber of Commerce (899-8118) for a walking tour guide of the town's historic district.

The inn's entrees start at $8.95 and run to $22.45 (a la carte); rooms for two range from $48 to $55. All prices are subject to change and are provided only for comparison.

Jacksonville Inn
175 East California Street
Jacksonville, OR 97530
(503) 899-1900

Morrison's Lodge

Morrison's Lodge is unique. It stands alone in wilderness experiences, combining homey touches of country and generous portions of nature.

Its setting alone is enough to make the lodge a winner. Towering evergreens and stately oaks shade the wilderness from the hot southern Oregon sun. Steep forested bluffs form a rolling horizon. Breezes whisper through the pines; a deer nibbles grass. Overhead, a pair of eagles soars upon the currents.

Belying its reputation, the mighty Rogue River maintains a low profile. Here the black waters do little more than ripple. The river displays only a touch of froth as it washes around a bend, cascading over a cadre of rocks. But its gentle rhythm is only a charade. Its peaceful repose represents merely a pause – an opportunity to gather strength before plunging headlong toward the Pacific.

Only a mile downriver, at Grave Creek Falls, the river boils and rages. It thunders over sheer drops, leaving rafters breathless. For another 50 miles it pulses with energy. It is this spirit which draws rafters to its banks. In late spring and throughout the summer the Rogue's waters often turn orange with rubber inflatables.

Then in fall the Rogue vibrates with another kind of energy. This is when steelhead, migratory rainbow trout ranging from one-half to ten pounds in weight, return to the river. From September through November anglers seeking sport replace rafters searching for adventure.

In the midst of this wilderness sits the log lodge and stilted cottages of Morrison's. Looking out upon a quiet stretch of the Rogue and trimmed in red, the cabins and two cozy rooms in the main lodge host rafters and anglers, as well as bicyclists, hikers and those just looking to get away. From May through mid-November guests congregate at this riverside resort.

The motel-like cottage units (raised on spars since the flood of 1964) include both housekeeping suites (with living rooms, kitchens and two bedrooms) and one-bedroom accommodations. Each cabin is comfortably furnished and features air conditioning, color television, a fireplace, a deck and a covered carport. All facilities have private bathrooms.

Like all of the region's very best places, the people here make the difference. Owners B.A. and Elaine Hanten each provide their own brand of hospitality. Broad-shouldered and forthright, with a down-to-earth sense of humor, B.A. takes pleasure in sharing his first-hand knowledge of this back country, particularly the river. Elaine, gracious and vibrant, loves to share her cooking, which is indeed special, and her enthusiasm for the Rogue.

Food is prepared in a country kitchen and served family-style in the lodge's dining room. Dinner conversation winds around the long tables, while platters of tender beef, homemade pasta and fresh vegetables pass from hand to hand. Breakfast includes large servings of such dishes as home-baked biscuits, gravy, ham, bacon, eggs, fresh preserves, pulpy juice, tea and coffee.

For those who love the Northwest's back country and good old country hospitality, Morrison's is, to quote a recent guest, "simply the best."

Travel Notes and Insider Tips

Take I-5 to the Merlin exit, about four miles north of Grants Pass. Follow Galice Road west about 12 miles through Merlin. Morrison's Lodge is on the right. By airplane, fly into Medford. Make arrangements with the lodge for pickup.

The Hantens can arrange day trips ($175 per boat, up to six adults), four-day camping trips ($325 per person) and three-day lodge trips ($350 per person) down the Rogue. The cost includes everything. During fishing season the lodge provides licensed guides (guide charges paid separately). Fishing equipment can be furnished. For both fishing and rafting, check with the lodge for specific details. Stop by the Grants Pass Chamber of Commerce (476-7717) for a detailed brochure of the myriad activities available within a few hours' drive, including the Oregon Caves, the Redwood National Park, Crater Lake and a variety of scenic drives.

Lodge rates vary from housekeeping ($66 for two, food not included) to summer American ($55 per person, breakfast and dinner included). From September 15th to closing, rates are $90 per person (includes breakfast, lunch and dinner). The lodge doesn't have a liquor license, but guests are welcome to bring their own. October is the most difficult time to get a reservation. All rates are subject to change and are provided only for comparison.

Morrison's Lodge
8500 Galice Road
Merlin, OR 97532
(503) 476-3825

Portland

Portland's skyscrapers rise above a cozy city that delights in its livability. While Mt. Hood glistens on the eastern horizon, Portlanders stroll up and down bricked Fifth and Sixth Avenues, the broad streets that make up the city's bus-only transit mall. Here the absence of cars spewing gray pollutants and blaring raspy horns permits shopping in an environment designed for people rather than machines.

Unlike many modern metropolitan areas, Portland is a city that measures growth in acres of parks and gardens instead of towering monoliths. In all, there are some 7,500 acres of parks, including the world's smallest – 24-inch-wide Mill Ends Park – and America's largest urban wilderness – 5,000-acre Forest Park. Portland's gardens blossom year-round. The Chamber claims the city supports more garden clubs per capita than any other American metropolis. The city's grandest garden, the formal Japanese Garden, overlooks downtown from its Washington Park perch. Since 1907, the city of roses has honored its green thumb with the Portland Rose Festival, held annually in June.

Despite its inland location, Portland is a waterfront city. It pokes its shoulder into the southern confluence of the mighty Columbia and the gray Willamette. So, in many ways, the city's economy has traveled on the decks of foreign ships. This resulted in a somewhat ribald past that translated into a rough-and-tumble waterfront. In the 1800s it abounded with seedy bars, dives and alleys, which catered to ships' crews. However, these days verdant Waterfront Park and modern developments characterize the banks of the Willamette as it courses through Portland's heart.

A large portion of Portland's economic base still plies the murky waters, but sophistication and culture do roam the mainland. Dozens of art galleries dot downtown streets. The most impressive, with a permanent collection of more than 18,000 works, is the Portland Art Museum. Within short walking distances of the museum stand several more bastions of culture, including the Center for the Performing Arts (241-0788), featuring the 2,800-seat Arlene Schnitzer Concert Hall; the Portland Civic Auditorium (248-4496), built in 1918 and home to the Portland Opera; and the Oregon Historical Center, a gold mine of Pacific Northwest lore.

Like all cities, Portland is growing and changing. However, the pace is tempered by concern for the human condition. Portland's "livable" reputation has been earned and continues to dominate the thoughts of the city's movers and shakers.

Travel Notes and Insider Tips

Portland sits at the crossroads of I-5 and I-84 and is easily accessed by automobile. Portland International Airport is only a 15-minute drive from downtown.

No stay in Portland would be complete without a visit to the following sites: Japanese Garden (223-1321); Portland Art Museum (226-2811); Lawrence Gallery (224-9442), presenting many of the Northwest's finest artists; Washington Park Zoo (226-1561); Oregon Museum of Science and Industry (222-2828); the Forestry Center (228-1367), showcasing Oregon's timberlands; Oregon Historical Center (222-1741); Pittock Mansion (248-4469), a historic home that commands great views; the transit mall; and Waterfront Park (796-5193), overlooking the Willamette.

Be sure to pack comfortable walking shoes (this city is best toured on foot) and don't forget rain gear (Portland experiences about 150 days of moist weather every year). For more information write or call: Greater Portland Convention and Visitors Association, 26 S.W. Salmon Street, Portland, OR 97204, (222-2223). All of the above telephone numbers are in area code 503.

Alexis

It's hard to decide what to like most about the Alexis. Everything here, from the location to the service, seems custom designed to achieve the ultimate goal of a first-class hotel – guest comfort.

The making of every successful hotel, whether it's in Portland or Paris, begins with a prime location. Even a grand palace would have trouble attracting guests if it were stuck out in a far-away suburb or a noisy neighborhood. Urban visitors expect convenience; they want easy access to downtown stores, to theaters, galleries and business centers. So hotels congregate around those areas, joining other faceless monoliths in mountain ranges of glass and steel. Concrete, not water, usually laps at their lobbies.

From the very beginning the Alexis held an advantage over its competitors, boasting not only a central location but also a waterfront perch. The worldly traveler may even feel as if they have been whisked off to Chicago's voguish Lake Shore Drive.

With the gray waters of the Willamette River rippling past, the four-story hotel stands on the edge of downtown. Its 83-foot-wide rotunda roof casts long shadows over the sloping lawns of Waterfront Park and its turrets look out on RiverPlace, a neighborhood of wood-frame condominiums and private courtyards.

Having a great location lures guests, but it takes more than a view to induce them to return. Service, amenities and decor make up the ingredients that draw travelers back time and time again. Like its older sibling in Seattle, the Portland Alexis features plenty of each.

Service begins with a no-tipping policy and a philosophy which says guests deserve the best. "We don't say no," Todd Johnson, General Manager, explains. "If our guests need something we will get it for them. Our guests should always feel as if they're staying in a fine residence, with a group of friends who want to make them happy."

This attitude is apparent from the moment travelers pull up to valet parking. Wearing a shiny black top hat and leather gloves, the doorman flashes a smile and a greeting, while the smartly dressed bell captain assists with the luggage. Service is prompt, cordial, efficient and unmotivated by greed. Throughout the hotel, from the clerks at the marbled front desk to the waiters in the Esplanade Restaurant, the staff coddles their guests.

The hotel's menu of amenities reads like a sybarite's shopping list. It starts with valet parking, then an inquiry by the front desk as to the newspaper desired for morning delivery. Complimentary sherry awaits in the guest rooms along with terry robes, down pillows, telephone extensions in the bathrooms, designer toiletries, digital clocks and remote control televisions. In addition, some of the suites offer fireplaces, refrigerators stocked with complimentary soft drinks, and whirlpool baths. Complimentary continental breakfasts and complimentary shoeshines are standard fare for all accommodations.

Looking more like a European resort or a great Californian mansion than an in-city hotel, the Alexis features an interior design which complements its residential appearance. In the common areas, large windows naturally illuminate muted colors, oak wainscoting, wood trim, tile and marble fireplaces, plush carpets, antique tables, overstuffed furniture, potted palms and grand floral displays. The 74 rooms, which wrap U-shaped around an inner courtyard, carry on the mood. In fact, the accommodations reflect a homey ambiance often sought by hotels but seldom achieved.

Since its opening the Seattle Alexis has ranked as that city's best small hotel. On November 4, 1985, the Portland Alexis welcomed its first guests. Its premiere marked the arrival of Portland's first great small luxury hotel.

Travel Notes and Insider Tips

From I-5, south-bounders should take the City Center Exit to the Front Avenue Exit. Then follow the signs to I-5 south before turning left onto Harbor Way. North-bounders should also take the City Center Exit (299B). Then take the Front Avenue Exit, turn right onto Montgomery, then an immediate left onto Harbor Way.

The Alexis makes up part of a new development called RiverPlace. The neighborhood includes restaurants, a health and fitness center, a marina and a shopping arcade. The Shanghai Club, at the end of the arcade, is an upbeat place to have a drink and listen to music. Three blocks from the hotel sits the Portland Convention and Visitors Bureau, the Portland Carousel Museum and the Yamhill Historic District. In the District, visit the Yamhill Marketplace for fresh fruits and vegetables and Partners In Time for rugs and antiques.

All of the rooms at the Alexis are good choices. Besides being light and airy, they are all spacious. However, views vary: City views are interesting, water views are outstanding. Courtyard rooms should be chosen by those who care little about views, although the yard is very pleasant. The Alexis Suites (bedroom and sitting area) represent the hotel's best bargains, but the Fireplace Suites are its best rooms. Rates for a double run from $115 to $130 for a standard, from $130 to $150 for an Alexis Suite, from $160 to $180 for a Parlor Suite (separate living room), and $225 for a Fireplace Suite. The Grand Suite costs $500. Fare at the Esplanade is regional seasonal and features such main dishes as duck with red currant sauce, salmon with leeks and mussels and sturgeon with Pernod sauce. Entrees range from $12.50 to $21.95. All prices are subject to change and are provided only for comparison.

Alexis
1510 S.W. Harbor Way
Portland, OR 97201
(503) 228-3233
(800) 227-1333 (Outside Oregon)

The Westin Benson

Cities lean heavily upon the shoulders of their pasts and inherit sustenance from legacies left by caring citizens. Simon Benson filled these roles as a Portland benefactor. Some 40 years after his death, the "Northwest Lumber King" still pulses through the city's lifeblood.

Bronze fountains, donated by Benson, dot downtown street corners; Benson Polytechnic School, partially financed by Benson, still educates Portland students; and the nearby Benson State Park continues to welcome picnickers. Yet it is The Westin Benson which perhaps best illustrates this patron's devotion to commerce and his desire to attract tourism and business to Portland.

The hotel's first guests checked in on April 22, 1914. Known then as The Benson, in honor of its owner, the hotel immediately became a Portland landmark. In 1981, amidst some controversy, the hotel's name was changed to The Westin Benson to reflect its current ownership.

Today, a red-helmeted doorman greets guests at the S.W. Broadway entrance. Rising above the sidewalk, twelve stories of white stone and terra-cotta brick clothe the French baroque-style building. A mansard roof serves as its elegant chapeau.

Inside the lobby, sunlight filters through large windows, draped Palladian-style. Polished Circassian walnut, imported from Imperial Russia, dresses the columns and panels the walls. Cut-glass chandeliers suspend from the plaster coffered ceiling. A veined marble fireplace trimmed in gold neighbors an Italian marble staircase fringed by a cast-iron railing.

Registration with the uniformed desk clerk is expedient and courteous but somewhat formal. Corporate travelers should feel at home with the business-like manner; however, leisure travelers may be intimidated by the appearance of stuffiness. They shouldn't be! The hotel is comfortable and other staff members do not scrimp on smiles.

Each of the 321 guest rooms has been renovated within the past three years. Soft peach and jade green color schemes enhance custom-designed furniture. Lithographs by Portland artist Judy Kinney Tidrick garnish the walls. Telephones and color televisions are customary amenities as well as shelves of designer toiletries.

Accommodations range in size from standard to suite. Skip the standard rooms unless $15 means a lot or there are no other rooms available: Standards are small and suitable only for sleeping. The penthouse rooms are spacious, comfortable and reasonably priced but not as chic as their title. An elegant suite can be booked for $70 more or a roomy deluxe for $60 less. Corporate rates are available to the business traveler.

Two restaurants call The Westin Benson home – The London Grill and Trader Vic's. In 1985, "Travel/Holiday" magazine awarded The London Grill a fine dining recommendation, which means in simple terms that guests can expect a consistently good meal. By any standards, however, The London Grill ranks as one of Portland's finer eating establishments.

Located in the hotel's lower level, the Grill breathes atmosphere. A 1793 English polished steel fireplace garnished with mirrors adorns one wall. Oak paneling, curved ceilings, brass torch lamps and tasteful chandeliers surround diners. In addition to seasonal specialties, the Grill's fare features entrees ranging from roast rack of lamb with peanut and herb crust to boneless Oregon trout with walnut herb butter.

Much of the hotel's business is corporate or involves meetings. To service the needs of these guests, the hotel offers a variety of elegant meeting rooms, from the expansive ballroom, capable of seating 800, to the cozy executive rooms, just right for 20 to 50 people. Its central location makes the hotel convenient to several local corporate headquarters.

Every element of this hotel – extravagant and elegant decor, smartly dressed staff and expert service – radiates style. It is among the best that Portland has to offer.

Travel Notes and Insider Tips

Broadway is a major downtown boulevard and is easily accessed from I-5. From either direction drivers should take the City Center Exit. Be aware that Broadway travels only one way – south.

Street-side rooms on the hotel's lower floors are subject to noise during the day, but it calms as evening turns to night. The tenth floor is for non-smokers only. Turndown service is available upon request as are major daily newspapers. Complimentary coffee and tea are served in the lobby in the mornings from 5:30 to 6:30 and in the afternoons from 2:30 to 4:30. Ask the concierge for a "walk, ride, drive guide" to the Portland area.

Double rates begin at $91; suites start at $250. The London Grill's entrees range from $14.75 to $22.25. All prices are subject to change and are provided only for comparison.

**The Westin Benson
S.W. Broadway at Oak
Portland, OR 97205
(503) 228-9611
(800) 228-3000 (Inside the United States and Canada)**

The Heathman Hotel

Since December 17, 1927, when the original 225-room Heathman received praise as "Portland's newest and most modern hotel," generations of Portlanders have held a special spot in their hearts for this landmark. In addition to once being a popular meeting place for Portland's families, the hotel also played a significant role as a host on Broadway's "Great White Way," the city's theatrical district and hotel center. This helped to elevate the ten-story Italian Renaissance structure to stardom. But by the 1960s the hotel's star, like other aging Broadway glitters, was fading to black.

Then in 1982 the Stevenson family purchased the hotel. Two years and $16 million later, a restored and renewed Heathman sparkled once again. Today, as in days past, the hotel shares a shiny image with its renovated neighbor, the Arlene Schnitzer Concert Hall. The Hall (formerly the Paramount Theatre) is the centerpiece of Portland's Center for the Performing Arts. The Heathman both enjoys and promotes this linkage with the arts.

"We're very actively seeking the entertainment-oriented traveler who wants to come to Portland on the weekend and play," Tim Nugent, sales representative, says.

The Heathman's closeness to the Center offers rare convenience to theater patrons. However, there is much more. The hotel also poses within walking distance of the Portland Art Museum, movie theaters, art galleries, jazz clubs and the Transit Mall.

Art also plays an important role in the hotel's design scheme. Nearly one percent of the Heathman's renovation budget adorns the hotel's walls. Mark and Francie Stevenson joined Elizabeth Leach of Portland's Elizabeth Leach Gallery in putting together the collection.

"My goal was to collect a representational selection of the very best by Pacific Northwest artists," Elizabeth explains. "We sought to purchase unique works on both paper and canvas.

"The idea of the Heathman is to be the best," she continues. "The nature of the hotel is quality. The art reflects that same quality and exquisite taste which the owners of the Heathman have and expect."

The brilliance of the works displayed here stands unsurpassed by any other regional hotel. Nevertheless, the Heathman's true masterpiece lies in its ambiance – its supereminent decor, its impeccable management and its superlative service. As a result, hotel guests are treated with a style and finesse which transcends travelers' expectations.

The Heathman is ideally suited for both the corporate executive and the leisure traveler. Both will discover first-class accommodations within elegant surroundings which exude personality.

High walls clad with rich Burmese teak adorn the cozy lobby, where even registration proves a pleasant experience. There is no hubbub of conventioneers (the hotel's small size and its intimate meeting rooms discourage large gatherings); desk clerks elevate friendly efficiency to new heights; and bellhops handle luggage as if it were delicate porcelain.

Adjacent to the lobby sits the lounge, which mirrors the hotel's original interior. With the exception of the white Carrara marble fireplace and two classic oil paintings by Claude Joliett, which originally hung in Windsor Palace, much looks the same as it did some 60 years ago. A warmth radiates from Australian eucalyptus gumwood paneling; a grand stairway trimmed with an iron balustrade climbs to the mezzanine; light flows gently through arched windows of frosted glass; classical and sentimental melodies cascade from the ebony Steinway; and marble tables mingle with brass lamps to complete the aesthetic balance.

During renovation the new owners reduced the number of rooms to 160. Forty of them are suites; each accommodation honors taste. San Francisco's Andrew Delfino melded warm earth tones, McGuire rattan, Roman travertine, Burmese teak and brass trim to create a deco style which soothes rather than overwhelms. Match-stick blinds cast angular shadows across marble tabletops; brass lamps garnish dark-stained end tables; English chintz covers king-sized beds; and green plants add a breath of freshness.

Coffered ceilings, red and black marble, etched glass and teak paneling grace the 86-seat tiered restaurant.

An extensive wine list, featuring Northwest, California, French, German and Italian wines, complements a seasonally varied menu distinguished by Pacific Northwest seafood and game. The preparation of each dish is superb and the presentation exquisite.

The Heathman's stature as a fine mid-size hotel is growing. Travelers who care about quality can only hope for more hotels such as this one.

Travel Notes and Insider Tips

From I-5, drivers traveling in either direction should take the City Center Exit east to Broadway. Portland International is only a few minutes away.

Don't miss afternoon tea in the lobby lounge. Serving days are Tuesday, Wednesday, Thursday and Saturday from 2:00 to 5:00. The hotel features a complimentary movie library with a wonderful selection of films which, upon request of the front desk, will be piped into your room. Check with the hotel about theater packages. The concierge is a great resource for business, social and recreational needs. The hotel features first-class meeting rooms for groups under 140.

Doubles begin at $90 for guest rooms, $110 for junior suites and $190 for suites. Dinner entrees average about $16.95. All prices are subject to change and are provided only for comparison.

The Heathman Hotel
S.W. Broadway at Salmon
Portland, OR 97205
(503) 241-4100
(800) 551-0011 (Inside the United States)

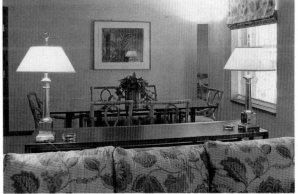

Tu Tú Tun Lodge

Tu Tú Tun bridges two worlds – the scenic beauty of Oregon's southern coast and the untamed wilderness of the Rogue River. In doing so the lodge creates an environment attractive to both adventurous visitors and leisure travelers. It accomplishes this feat of lodging magic with warmth and style.

Located seven miles up the north side of the Rogue River from the seacoast community of Gold Beach, the lodge's two cedar buildings overlook the Rogue's meandering waters. To the south, rolling hills rise above the wide rippling river. A golden sun chases shadows across the horizon and breezes bearing the sea waft across the grounds.

At Tu Tú Tun fishing tops a long list of adventures. Freshwater anglers know the Rogue by reputation. It is one of only three Oregon rivers that boast a spring salmon run. But it is in fall that the river jumps to life. From September through October it teems with steelhead and Chinook. For those who prefer ocean action to the river rock, surf and deep sea fishing beckon from the Pacific. Charter boats depart regularly from Gold Beach.

While some come for the fishing, others look forward to speeding up the Rogue aboard a jet boat. Both a 64-mile and a 104-mile trip are available. The longer adventure splashes through the river's white-water wilderness amidst forested mountain country sheltering bears, eagles, deer and osprey. The charges run from $22.50 to $45 per person.

Hikers, beachcombers and golfers find plenty to do as well. Humbug Mountain Trail, a 45-minute drive north, climbs through evergreen forests and fields of wildflowers; nearby Cape Sebastian features sandy beaches, clam digging and ocean panoramas; and Cedar Bend Golf Course offers nine holes just 15 minutes from the lodge.

A more relaxing agenda presents itself along the coast. Scenic drives up and down Highway 101 between Port Orford to the north and Brookings to the south afford spectacular Pacific views: deep coves swirling with froth, sun-splashed beaches glittering under blue skies and rocky monoliths jutting through blue-green waves.

Back at Tu Tú Tun, owners Dirk and Laurie Van Zante provide pampering in a friendly atmosphere. Guests lodge either in one of 16 rooms making up the two-story rectangular guest house or one of two upstairs river suites in the main lodge. The guest house units feature two double beds, a sitting area, carpeting, fresh flowers, balconies or patios, private bathrooms and river views. The spacious suites boast living rooms and dining areas, fully equipped kitchens, bedrooms with two double beds, and roomy bathrooms. River Suite One also has a sunny deck and a wood-burning stove.

Dinner is special. An old school bell rings one-half hour early, calling guests to congregate in the main lodge for complimentary hors d'oeuvres and friendly conversation. Dirk and Laurie greet every guest by their first name and before long the gathering takes on aspects of a

family reunion. At dinner-time Dirk seats guests family-style. The four-course dinner, featuring set-entrees of regional specialties, is then served by Dirk and Laurie.

Tu Tú Tun Lodge rated four stars in the 1984 "Mobil Travel Guide," and "USA Today" called it "one of the 16 most inviting inns in the nation." It is definitely one of the region's best lodges.

Travel Notes and Insider Tips

The lodge is open from May 1st to November 1st. Car access is from Highway 101. Turn east on North Bank Rogue just north of the Rogue River Bridge on the outskirts of Gold Beach. Follow signs seven miles to the river's edge. Gold Beach Airport has a 3,200-foot-long paved and lighted runway. The lodge provides pickup service.

Gold Beach is a full-service seaside community that offers legalized gambling. Be sure to bring a camera and lots of film – photo opportunities abound on the river and along the coast. Wear warm layers of clothing for river adventures. Tu Tú Tun is popular and reservations can be difficult. Make plans several months in advance.

Doubles range from $77 to $95; breakfast costs $5.50 and dinner $16.50 per person. All prices are subject to change and are provided only for comparison.

Tu Tú Tun Lodge
96550 North Bank Rogue
Gold Beach, OR 97444
(503) 247-6664

Salishan Lodge

The Oregon seacoast receives oceans of praise for its sun-soaked beaches, deep coves, rocky headlands and steep bluffs that look out on miles of ocean blue. From the Columbia to the Rogue, state and federal officials protect these unspoiled coastlands like lionesses mothering their cubs.

In some instances, however, private individuals who own small stretches of the coast have ravaged Oregon's beauty in the name of profitability. As a result, a few communities bear the scars of honky-tonk capitalism – neon signs flashing fast food and sprawling rectangular boxes marking motels.

In the early 1960s Oregon millionaires John D. and Betty Gray, who love this environment, resolved to stop the rape of the land. They searched for a delicate balance – one that would preserve the integrity of the environment yet allow visitors to bathe in its splendor. In 1965 their labor of love gave birth to Salishan Lodge, the standard for first-class resorts in the Northwest.

Salishan is a portrait of a pristine environment. Nestled in a forested slope overlooking the Pacific, the 700-acre resort complements the landscape. General Manager

Hank Hickox explains: "Salishan is a product of the environment and is very understated. It doesn't jump out at you but, instead, creeps out of the hills."

Ecology played such an important role in the lodge's development that it produced the resort's only drawback: Salishan's waterfront splashes one-half mile away. However, because of the developer's concern Salishan Peninsula remains well-conserved, and guests have access to miles of wide private beach.

Surrounded by windblown firs, hemlocks and spruces, Salishan's natural cedar buildings make a quiet statement. Covered walkways of spruce and cedar meander across the hills, connecting each building to the main lodge. Salal, ferns and rhododendron flourish beside other native plants, carpeting the grounds in a sea of green. Across the highway, Siletz Bay tucks its shoulder into the wooded finger of Salishan Peninsula. Further west the white-capped Pacific fades into the horizon, where it touches pale blue skies.

The Northwest theme also reigns in each of the resort's 151 rooms. Although sophisticated and moneyed travelers frequent Salishan, the ambiance cannot be labeled posh. A former manager described the scene as "quietly elegant." The decor walks in step with the idea of preserving and even representing the environment: cedar boards panel the walls, rough-hewn hemlock covers the canted ceilings, brick fireplaces remove the chill and works of art depict life along the coast. To permit every guest an opportunity to appreciate the beauty, each room offers either a water, forest or golf view.

Those seeking an outdoor experience in an environment that coddles will love Salishan. Guests swap their custom-made suits and designer dresses for hiking boots, tennis shorts, golf gloves and fishing hats. Nature trails snake through the hills and along Salishan Peninsula; the Salishan Tennis Club features three indoor courts with plexi-pave surfaces; an 18-hole championship golf course rolls amidst forests, dunes and sea; and ocean, stream and lake fishing beckon anglers. In addition, the lodge has an indoor recreation center that features a heated pool, hydrotherapy pool, men's and women's saunas, completely equipped gym and a private sunbathing patio.

As guests might expect dining is taken seriously here. Early evening sun cascades through the large windows of Salishan's Gourmet Room. Tables peer out across the emerald slopes falling gently toward the bay; in the distance Cascade Head rises in a veil of blue haze. As dusk chases the sun, candles flicker inside cranberry shades surrounded by crystal and china garnishing white linen tablecloths.

The smart service is impeccable. Knowledgeable waiters clad in black ties and jackets present a menu that includes a balanced variety of Continental and American

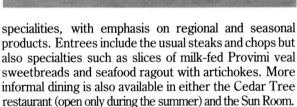

specialities, with emphasis on regional and seasonal products. Entrees include the usual steaks and chops but also specialties such as slices of milk-fed Provimi veal sweetbreads and seafood ragout with artichokes. More informal dining is also available in either the Cedar Tree restaurant (open only during the summer) and the Sun Room.

The fare is consistently good, although not always exciting. On the other hand, Salishan's wine cellar ranks among the best in North America. Phil DeVito, Salishan's celebrated cellarmaster and Oregon's premier sommelier, developed the resort's wine list over the past two decades. The wine cellar, which is available for tours four to six days a week, contains 30,000 bottles, while the wine list boasts 1,100 fine selections.

Winning the "Mobil Travel Guide's" Five-Star Award has become an annual event at Salishan. Once Oregon's best-kept secret, the lodge now attracts guests from throughout the United States and Canada. The reason is clear: Salishan Lodge leads the way in first-class pampering.

Travel Notes and Insider Tips

Salishan is located on U.S. 101 between Lincoln City and Depoe Bay. A 3,000-foot paved runway is available at nearby Siletz Bay State Airport. The Lodge is 95 miles southwest of Portland.

The resort's conference facilities and services are some of the finest in the Northwest. Conferences make up much of Salishan's business between September and June. Total function room space is over 14,000 square feet and accommodates groups from 12 to 500. Dress at the resort is informal, except in the Gourmet Room. The Oregon Coast is damp and cool, so be prepared. Salishan's art collection, featuring the works of Northwest artists, is superb. The best room views are from Chieftain House North; the best vista is from atop Cascade Head.

Room rates are seasonal and subject to discounts but generally range from $72 (forest view) to $136 (bay view) for a double. Entrees in the Gourmet Room range from $12 to $25. All prices are subject to change and are provided only for comparison.

Salishan Lodge
Gleneden Beach, OR 97388
(503) 764-3600 (Reservations)
(503) 764-3605 (Conference Information)

New Surfview Resort

Sand and sunset – one drenched in sun, the other bidding a sanguine farewell to its glory – pose outside the windows of the New Surfview Resort.

Under the watchful gaze of Haystack Rock, the resort's three-story shake-clad structures perch atop a grass-covered bluff. Below, along the white sands of Cannon Beach, worshipers of sun, surf and sand relax upon colorful beach blankets, bounce over white crests of foamy waves and fling Frisbees into the salt air.

As day fades to dusk, a reddish orange pattern streaks across the horizon. Wisps of clouds spread fingers of color toward the darkened shore. Couples stroll in shadow against the rolling sea. It takes several hours for a black curtain to finally fall over the scene.

Many of the resort's 105 guest rooms look out on this seaside scenery. However, the views vary from panoramas (Ocean Front) to peeks (Ocean View). There are even a few rooms where windows peer out only on shrubs. Inside, the accommodations range from spa units with kitchenettes to cozy standards. All rooms feature fireplaces and private bathrooms; most offer lanais.

In addition to the resort's ocean-front setting, amenities include an indoor pool, swirl-spas, a sauna and exercise room. There are also covered parking and daily door delivery of the "Oregonian."

The Surfview Too Restaurant, located across Hemlock Street, opened the summer of 1984. Directors' chairs surround wooden tables amidst sun-splashed hanging plants, while brass railings and cedar trim garnish the comfortable environment. Steaks and seafood headline the fare.

Tiny Cannon Beach, home of the famous summer sand castle contest, mirrors many East Coast resort communities – motels line the streets as do gift shops and restaurants; bungalows form a long gray line along the beach. Nevertheless, the tree-lined mountains of Oregon's Coast Range provide a seclusion travelers seldom discover along the Atlantic.

The New Surfview's seaside location, its informal comfort and its nearness to Portland and Seattle combine to make this resort an excellent choice for either summer fun or winter storm-watching.

Travel Notes and Insider Tips

From Portland take U.S. 26 to Highway 101 south to Cannon Beach. From Seattle follow I-5 south to Longview, then 432 to Oregon's U.S. 30. In Astoria drive south on U.S. 101. The resort is located on the southern edge of downtown Cannon Beach, just 30 miles south of Astoria.

Bring warm clothes. The Oregon Coast can be cool year-round. The beach and scenery are the main attractions here. The sand castle contest is held in June. Offshore breezes ensure good kite-flying conditions year-round. Shopping is a sidelight. White Bird Gallery in Cannon Beach has an excellent collection of crafts. Nearby Seaside features an array of gift shops as well as an arcade for the younger crowd.

Double rates range from $75 to $135 in season; winter rates are considerably lower. Restaurant entrees range from $6.95 to $17.95. In the summer, room reservations should be made several months in advance. All prices are subject to change and are provided only for comparison.

New Surfview Resort
1400 South Hemlock
Cannon Beach, OR 97110
(503) 436-1566
(800) 452-7132 (Inside Oregon)
(800) 547-6423 (Outside Oregon)

Channel House

The sun washes through the haze and shimmers off the blue-green waters of the Pacific. Frothy waves splash upon the rocks, leaving black tidal pools in their wake. To the north, a rolling headland juts into the sea. Atop the promontory windblown firs shadow clapboard houses.

Sitting atop a steep perch, 25 feet above the swirling waters, the Channel House oversees this parcel of Oregon coastline. Since 1980, when owner Paul Schwabe saved the two-story gray-shingled building from the wrecking ball, this tiny inn has been serving bed and breakfast to Depoe Bay visitors.

Rooms three and five share star billing here. Both are ocean suites with private decks, fireplaces, kitchens and whirlpool baths. Their decor borders on simple, but their views garner five stars: It's like sailing a yacht into the sunset without the seasickness.

The remaining five accommodations feature only sneak previews of the ocean scenery. Rooms four and six offer the best peeks, with number four also looking downtown. Number seven (which is not available in winter) features a kitchenette; numbers one and two are cozy first-floor abodes.

All the rooms share a common appointment – thin walls. As in most small inns, especially those reaching senior-citizen status, noise ignores the restraints of slender partitions. Fortunately, guests understand this and Johnny Carson's voice seldom intrudes on sleeping neighbors.

Breakfast, which is included in the rates, eases the pain of rising from a comfortable cocoon. Greg and Freda, innkeepers, prepare a sumptuous repast. Typically, guests savor quiche, apple roll-up, seasonal fruit, home-baked muffins, pulpy juice and steaming coffee or tea.

In addition to accommodations, the inn houses an oyster bar and restaurant. Ships' wheels and ocean-going artifacts trimmed with brass dot its red brick floor. A Pacific view accompanies each entree, which range from Oysters Channel House (baked with tomato sauce, mozzarella cheese, sautéed green peppers and onions) to sautéed sole almondine.

The town of Depoe Bay boasts "the smallest navigable harbor in the world." The village's Main Street isn't much bigger, but it is charming and quaint. Depoe Bay is a town of saltwater taffy, clam chowder and sea breezes.

Travel Notes and Insider Tips

U.S. 101 is also Main Street, Depoe Bay. Look for Channel House just south of the bridge, alongside the ocean, one block off the highway.

Consider an off-season visit. It is a terrific spot for watching both migrating gray whales and immigrating winter storms. Both arrive between early December and late May. For fishing ocean salmon season usually begins in mid-May and runs to mid-September. There are five charter offices in Depoe Bay. Don't miss the views at Cape Foulweather, just south of town.

Room rates range from $35 to $120 a night for a double; restaurant entrees run between $9.95 and $14.95. All prices are subject to change and are provided only for comparison.

**Channel House
P.O. Box 56
Depoe Bay, OR 97341
(503) 765-2140**

Rosebriar Inn

Like its hometown of Astoria, Rosebriar Inn boasts a long and colorful past. Today owners Ann Leenstra and Judith Papendick welcome guests to this refurbished home, encouraging visitors to enjoy the quiet ambiance of that earlier era.

Its history began in 1902 when Frank Patton, a local banker, built the house to serve as a private residence. The Patton family owned the building until 1951. Then the Archdiocese of Portland purchased the house and doubled its size to 7,000 square feet. Bearing the title "Holy Name Convent," the home housed 14 nuns until 1973, when it became a home for girls.

Following several periods of disuse during the late '70s and early '80s, the house made a comeback after it was purchased by the current owners. Seeing the potential for a bed-and-breakfast inn, Ann and Judith began tackling the task of transformation. Their major challenge entailed altering the home's institutional drabness: white walls upstairs and sepulchral emptiness downstairs.

First, the oak floors were given new life. Then rolls of wallpaper, dancing with delicate floral prints, covered the paint. Antiques and Oriental rugs arrived on the scene next. Finally, green plants and limited edition prints garnished everything.

Now the neoclassical Greek clapboard building beckons guests to relax in one of its cozy upstairs guest rooms, which border a long hallway. Tall old windows and miles of wood trim add a touch of character to accommodations already breathing gulps of personality. Most of the nine rooms share a dormitory-style hall bathroom; all have sinks.

Breakfast is served in the downstairs dining room. It is included in the rates and features a main dish, homemade banana bran muffins, fresh fruit, juice, Stash tea and Boyd coffee. Three brass chandeliers hang over a long dining table set atop Oriental carpets. Antique lace curtains and serving buffets reflect grandma's time, while green plants add a homey freshness to the leisurely meal.

Although bed and breakfasts, like all lodgings, are not for everyone, those who enjoy feeling at home on the road will enjoy their stay at Rosebriar.

Travel Notes and Insider Tips

Take either I-5 or Highway 101 to U.S. 30. Astoria is located in the northwest corner of Oregon at the mouth of the Columbia River. In Astoria go up 12th Street, turn left on Franklin to 14th.

Astoria, settled in 1811, was the first permanent American settlement on the Pacific Coast. To recall its past visit Fort Clatsop, four miles south of town on U.S. 101; Fort Astoria, located on Exchange Street; Clatsop County Historical Museum, perched on 8th Street; and the Columbia River Maritime Museum, sprawled along Marine Drive. The Scandinavian Midsummer Festival is held in June and the Astoria Regatta in August. The Ship Inn (325-0033) is a good place to have dinner. Contact the Astoria Area Chamber of Commerce (325-6311) for more information.

Double rates range from $36 to $48. Children under 12 are conditional; smoking is not welcome inside the house. All prices are subject to change and are provided only for comparison.

Rosebriar Inn
636 Fourteenth Street
Astoria, OR 97103
(503) 325-7427

Columbia Gorge Hotel

On its final rush to freedom, the Columbia River cuts a mighty swath through the Cascade Mountains. In the gorge's midst, just 60 miles from Portland, stands an elegant refuge: a getaway destination known as the Columbia Gorge Hotel.

Evenings at the hotel paint scenes like those portrayed in poems and songs by romantic lyricists. Silvery moonlight shimmers across black waters and shadowy heights rise into the dusk. Only the tumbling deluge of Wah-Gwin-Gwin Falls, cascading 200 feet from its hilltop fountainhead, interrupts the lucid stillness.

Atop a steep bluff, hurricane lamps flicker yellow from behind tall windows which grace the hotel's dining room. Inside, antique furniture, starched linens, floral arrangements, gleaming crystal and brass chandeliers adorn the River Terrace. Epicures dressed in East Coast sophistication sit alongside diners garbed in Northwest casual.

It is this freedom to relax, to be yourself amidst grand surroundings, which distinguishes this hotel. General Manager Glen T. Brydges explains: "Our main goal is to ensure that our guests have a pleasant time. We want to create an elegant environment of care and caring, where guests can be comfortable."

Looking like a Spanish parador, the Mediterranean-style villa poses within a sea of green. The hotel's tiled roof splashes burnt orange on the verdant surroundings, globular street lamps circle the drive, flower gardens imbue the grounds with dabs of color and a stream meanders under stone bridges.

The hotel lobby exudes a classic style – chandeliers, massive plastered beams, wing chairs and red-jacketed bellmen. The setting recalls the 1920s, when a burgeoning tourist industry inspired lumber baron Simon Benson to develop the Columbia Gorge Hotel. In 1921 Benson spent a half-million dollars constructing the resort. It welcomed the idle rich and attracted film stars such as Rudolph Valentino and Clara Bow.

Today, following some years of neglect during the '70s, the refurbished hotel reflects its earlier stylishness. The clientele seldom arrive in limousines these days, but they still enjoy the hotel's first-class environment.

In the dining room service is cordial and informative. Entrees range from fresh Columbia River salmon, to eastern Oregon double-thick lamb chops, to steak au poivre.

While evening dining is excellent, it is the complimentary four-course breakfast that has become regionally famous (although quantity may overshadow quality sometimes). The trademarked "World Famous Farm Breakfast" borders on decadence. It begins with a bounty of seasonal fruits and ends with a stack of buttermilk pancakes.

Comfort and simplicity mark the 46 guest rooms. Accommodations offer either river or garden views and double, queen- or king-size beds. Color schemes of rust, apricot, robin's-egg blue, gray or beige enhance the

rooms' aesthetic lines; plush carpets and window curtains soften decor; and spacious baths featuring designer toiletries provide modern conveniences.

Although the Columbia Gorge Hotel presents a picture of elegance, it resembles a country getaway. While the hotel's style leans toward sophistication, its location is strictly bucolic.

Travel Notes and Insider Tips

Portland International Airport is a 60-minute drive away. A small private field with a 3,000-foot runway, Hood River County Airport, is also nearby. In addition, Hood River is served by AMTRAK and Greyhound. By automobile take I-84, then Exit 62 for the hotel.

From June through September, an old-fashioned sternwheeler, the Columbia Gorge (223-3928), departs three times daily from sites along the river for two-hour scenic tours. Within an hour's drive of the hotel visit 620-foot Multnomah Falls, hike to the top of Larch Mountain for great mountain views, ski Mount Hood, fish on the river or at Lost Lake and receive a city-fix in Portland.

Room rates for a double range from $95 to $135; dinner entrees run from $12.95 to $19.95. Rooms with river views are best. There are also two roomy fireplace suites available. All prices are subject to change and are provided only for comparison.

Columbia Gorge Hotel
4000 West Cliff Drive
Hood River, OR 97031
(503) 386-5566

Flying M Ranch

The Flying M Ranch is back in the saddle again. Once more, automobile tires rumble across the four-mile gravel road which leads travelers to this guest ranch perched on the edge of Oregon's wine country.

During the 1970s and early 1980s, the Flying M resembled an ongoing family reunion. Visitors arrived from nearby Portland, made the five-hour drive from Seattle and flew in from all corners of the Northwest. These overnight guests joined locals and friends of owners Barbara and Bryce Mitchell for horseback rides along mountain trails, refreshing splashes in the pond, dining pleasures amongst rural trappings and spins around the Sawtooth Room's dance floor.

But then on January 3, 1983, tragedy struck. Fire licked at the two-story log Flying M lodge and by evening it consumed everything except the broad stone fireplace. "It would have been easy to give up," Barbara says. But the Mitchells didn't surrender to tragedy. On January 19, 1985, a new lodge made of mammoth Douglas firs opened.

Today the Flying M Ranch rides again. Meandering through the acreage, the North Yamhill River washes over its rocky bottom and splashes its banks. The dark, clear water courses through green leafy forests sheltering dozens of campsites, passes behind the blonde lodge housing restaurant and lounge, twists under a wooden footbridge, and whispers past private cabins and the 24-unit Bunkhouse Motel.

To the south, beyond the air strip which also masquerades as a meadow, horses shade themselves under covered corrals. Rising beyond the barns, thickly forested hills dressed in shades of green ramble beneath pale blue skies laced with swirls of white. Split-rail fences, wagon wheels and Western gates complete the picture.

"Our horses are our calling cards," Tom, Flying M's wrangler-guide, drawls. "They have one speed – slow. But it's the friendly atmosphere that makes this place work. We get lots of people who come here just because they've heard about Barbara and Bryce. It's right neighborly here. Everyone, guest and staff alike, is treated like a member of the family."

Lodging here is both modest and rustic. There are more than 100 campsites, 24 motel units (located in the Bunkhouse Motel) and two cabins made of rough-hewn boards. Dining is country as well – wholesome and plentiful but not gourmet.

The secret of Flying M's success rests in its friendly and Old West ambiance. It is a family operation. It is a getaway for people who like people.

Travel Notes and Insider Tips

The Flying M Ranch is located about 50 miles southwest of Portland, 10 miles west of Yamhill. From Portland take 99W to Newberg, then 240 to Yamhill. At this point you will need specific directions; even then you may think you are lost. But the drive is scenic and well worth the reward waiting at the end of the trail. There is also a 2,200-foot turf runway on the ranch.

The ranch offers miles of horseback riding trails and a varied list of riding choices. Overnight trail rides are available, including camping (mountain-cabin style) atop Trask Mountain. Rides range from as little as $8 an hour to $325 per person for a four-day mountain and beach excursion. The lodge houses two large function rooms – banquets, parties, workshops and meetings can be accommodated. The Flying M is only a short drive from several small vineyards. For a map of the wineries of Yamhill County write or call: McMinnville Chamber of Commerce, 417 North Adams, McMinnville, OR 97128 (472-6196).

Nightly rates for the motel units begin at $38; food is inexpensive. All prices are subject to change and are provided only for comparison.

Flying M Ranch
Route 1, Box 95C
Yamhill, OR 97148
(503) 662-3222

The Wayfarer Resort

The McKenzie River Valley courses an emerald path through Oregon's central Cascades and the Willamette National Forest. Cutting east from Eugene, the state's second largest city, Oregon Route 126 follows the McKenzie River as it winds through dense forests and tiny towns.

Located at the confluence of the McKenzie River and Marten Creek, The Wayfarer offers visitors to this pristine valley a cozy and comfortable getaway spot. Comfort is the key word here. All too often remote and peaceful hideaways within unspoiled surroundings feature too much rusticity. Although it can be rewarding and stimulating to commune with nature during the day, resort travelers usually prefer to relate to a comfortable sofa, a crackling fire and a warm bed at night. Most wish to leave nature outdoors as day fades to dusk. The Wayfarer does just that.

Each of the cabins boasts a modern kitchen and features electric heat, television and lots of hot water. Franklin stoves remove evening chills, while stuffed furniture relaxes vacationing bodies. Open-beam ceilings and pine paneling add touches of country. Other amenities include private decks, complete with barbecues and patio furniture; fresh flowers; and bowls of locally grown filberts.

The cabins range in size and views. Perched on the grounds away from the water sits the studio duplex unit, while seven one- and two-bedroom cottages nestle within the woods alongside Marten Creek. These units look out over the cold dark waters as they cascade down several low falls, ripple under a footbridge and wash over a rocky bed. In addition, a two-bedroom, two-bath cabin overlooks the confluence.

As well as the more secluded cabins, The Wayfarer features two larger homes and an apartment, which sit alongside the McKenzie. The Ol' Homestead houses four bedrooms and two and one-half baths, ideal for two families traveling together. On the other hand, the Octagon, which angles around a broad stone fireplace, offers two bedrooms, two baths, shag carpeting, a wet bar and a modern and fully equipped kitchen. The apartment ranks as the most modest facility here, with neither a stove nor a fireplace.

All of the facilities dot expansive grounds. To the south and west, the Cascade foothills roll above the resort. Evergreens, alders and maples flourish at The Wayfarer, casting shadows across the cedar structures. Manicured lawns descend to the banks of the river. Ducks swim in a pond, stocked with trout for young anglers, and a nearby wooden porch swing dangles from a vine-covered arbor. A gray stone driveway winds throughout the acreage.

The Wayfarer is a family resort. While it boasts many of the amenities of its bigger cousins, it is still small enough to offer the peace and quiet of a country inn.

Travel Notes and Insider Tips

Take I-5 to Eugene, then go east on Highway 126 twenty-five miles to the Goodpasture Covered Bridge. Cross the bridge and drive four miles. The resort is on the east side of Goodpasture Road.

In addition to tennis, volleyball, badminton, horseshoes and table tennis on the grounds, guests may fish from the banks of the McKenzie River for trout and steelhead. Although fishing from the banks is fun, boat fishing is better. Fishing guides, who can be reserved through The Wayfarer, are recommended. Costs for a couple start at $120 per day. Hiking and sightseeing opportunities in this area abound. Stop at the McKenzie Bridge Ranger Station for trail maps and information. The most scenic summer drive is the narrow twisting McKenzie Pass Highway (Route 242), which begins a few miles east of McKenzie Bridge and the ranger station. Tokatee Golf Club in Blue River boasts one of Oregon's most scenic 18-hole golf courses. No food is served at The Wayfarer; however, there are a few restaurants close by and Eugene is only a 35-minute drive away. Groceries for cabin preparation should be purchased at one of the large chain stores located on 126, just minutes from the interstate.

Accommodation rates per day start at $42 for a duplex unit and run up to $110 for either the Octagon or The Ol' Homestead. All prices are subject to change and are provided only for comparison.

The Wayfarer Resort
Star Route
Vida, OR 97488
(503) 896-3613

Black Butte Ranch

Perhaps the Northwest's most abused and overused word, "beautiful" is used to describe everything from the sun-splashed sands of the Oregon Coast, to the rolling plains of wheat in eastern Washington, to the jagged snowcapped peaks of British Columbia's Coast Mountains. Anyone who calls this region home or vacations here knows the magnificence of the landscape and the attractiveness of its getaways. Yet few places can match the unbridled grandeur of the environment making up Black Butte Ranch.

After entering through the manned main gate, a vast meadow unfolds. Horses and cows leisurely munch the grassland. In the near distance, beyond stands of ponderosa pine, rise the hills of the Deschutes National Forest and the summits of the Oregon Cascades.

Surrounded by this scenery, a black-topped drive meanders through Black Butte's 1,830 acres. It passes cedar-framed condominiums, which neighbor the lodge and the central recreation area. It winds past the Big Meadow Golf Course. Then the drive enters wooded home sites. Finally, it wraps around another 18-hole golf course, Glaze Meadow. Along the way the road passes tennis courts, swimming pools and 22 acres of spring-fed lakes.

Black Butte's accommodations vary greatly in space, decor and price. They range from the cozy standard and deluxe bedrooms, to spacious three-bedroom condominiums, to private homes available through the rental pool. The least expensive units, standard bedrooms, are aptly named: They are ordinary in every way, offering a bed, a shower and no view. The deluxes are the same small size but feature a full bath, a fireplace and a view.

All of the condominiums are roomy and come with fully equipped kitchens. The private homes boast forested privacy and elegant amenities.

Dining at the ranch equals any of the area's best restaurants. The environment is quiet. Tall pines shade the gray angular lodge, which houses the dining room. The tiered restaurant's design features several semiprivate nooks. Banks of windows look across a small lake dotting the wind-swept meadow; shadowy mountains serve as a towering backdrop. Large potted plants and fresh flowers pose below the open-beam canted ceiling. But it is the fare that matters. At Black Butte the food is prepared simply and tastes delicious, especially the roast prime ribs of beef au jus and the fresh trout. Be sure to save room for the just-baked sourdough chocolate cake.

As well as golf, tennis and swimming, activities abound in and around Black Butte. Adjacent to the lodge sits the Recreation Activity Center, where guests of all ages may enjoy such activities as ping pong, basketball, and arts and crafts. In addition, there is a playground for the youngsters. Other items on Black Butte's agenda include organized sports and games, hiking, rafting, fishing, canoeing, bicycling, cross-country skiing and horseback riding.

Portlanders, many of whom own homes here, have been in love with Black Butte since its conception in 1970. Now, however, the resort's reputation is spreading throughout the Northwest, making it a popular getaway amongst even far-away travelers.

Travel Notes and Insider Tips

The ranch is located eight miles west of Sisters on Highway 20. From I-5, exit Highway 20 east in Corvallis. The ranch is 134 miles southeast of Portland.

Reservations can be hard to come by from June 15 through September 15. During this period, two-night minimums for condominiums and four-night minimums for private homes are required. As well as making early reservations for accommodations, guests should consider making dinner reservations several days in advance. (They will not be accepted more than seven days ahead.) Summer reservations are also necessary for golf and tennis. For swimming or sunbathing, Paulina Pool is the least crowded and most secluded. Nearby Sisters is a quaint western town of square clapboard storefronts, with restaurants and gift shops. In the summer, visit the Dee Wright Observatory in McKenzie Pass (State 242 out of Sisters) for impressive views of lava fields and panoramas of the Cascades. On the way to the pass, stop and take a few pictures of the llamas at Patterson's Llama Ranch, just west of town. Hundreds of miles of hiking, cross-country skiing, snowshoeing and snowmobiling trails crisscross through the Deschutes National Forest. (Buy a map at the Sisters Ranger Station for detailed information.) Check with the resort about white-water rafting.

Rates range from $45 for a standard to $130 for a three-bedroom condominium. Private homes run from $80 to $130. Dinner entrees range from $9 to $22.50. All prices are subject to change and are provided only for comparison.

Black Butte Ranch
P.O. Box 8000
Black Butte Ranch, OR 97759
(503) 595-6211
(800) 452-7455 (Inside Oregon)

Rippling River Resort

Ruling over the Oregon Cascades, Mount Hood rises to a glaciated crest of 11,235 feet. Nestled within the mountain's shadow, Rippling River Resort hosts many of Hood's admirers. Skiers, hikers and sightseers flock to the resort year-round. Add mountain lakes for anglers, 27 challenging holes for golfers, six courts for tennis players and exercise facilities for fitness enthusiasts, and Rippling River earns its reputation as a recreational resort for all seasons.

Divided into two communities, East and West, the resort sprawls only minutes from the mountain's numerous charms. The forested Cascades ring the facilities with rolling ridges; the air smells of evergreen.

Accommodations here come in several sizes and shapes, from the condominiums at Rippling River East to the deluxe units at Rippling River West. All have an air of modesty about them but are roomy and comfortable.

The condominiums look out over the golf course and up at the Cascades. Large picture windows and private decks place the scenery close-up. Stone fireplaces dominate living rooms, dining areas neighbor kitchens and bedrooms border on spaciousness.

Eight two-story natural wood buildings, located near the main lodge and convention center, house the 132 deluxe units. Each unit is quiet and contains a private bathroom, color television and a telephone. The deluxe kings, Rippling River's best bargains, also feature fireplaces and continental kitchens.

Casual dining is available in the Pinehurst Family Dining Room, only a short putt from the 19th green. More elegant fare is served at the Forest Hills Dining Room in the main lodge.

Blue linen tablecloths, silk flowers, soft yellow candlelight and brass chandeliers set the mood at Forest Hills. Large windows look out on the shimmering turquoise waters of the pool, which is surrounded by shrubs and trees. The cuisine is strictly continental. While the food is good, the service is sometimes too relaxed and not always accommodating.

In fact, service is the one area that can be a drawback at the resort. Nevertheless, other than inconsistency in this area, Rippling River possesses all the ingredients of a first-class resort.

Recreation and relaxation make up its main components. The resort sits only 17 miles from North America's summer ski capital, Palmer Snowfield at Mount Hood's 8,500-foot level. In addition to year-round skiing at Palmer, Mount Hood Meadows and Mirror Mountain (formerly Multorpor Ski Bowl) offer terrain diversity and slope access just 25 miles and 12 miles away, respectively.

Hikers and climbers come from throughout North America to walk the Pacific Crest National Scenic Trail, winding through the Mount Hood National Forest, and to challenge Mount Hood's jagged peaks. Trout teem in both well-stocked lakes and the Salmon River, which also boasts steelhead runs.

The resort offers several special packages that help guests to take advantage of the environment. They include winter skiing; summer skiing and golf; fly-fishing; and a white-water raft adventure. The packages often feature items such as lodging, transportation, lift tickets, greens fees and guides.

Rippling River's new convention center provides facilities that can accommodate groups from ten to 1,000. The resort's marketing department handles reservations and information.

Mount Hood and the National Forest beckon visitors throughout the year. Rippling River can offer these travelers amenities and comfort.

Travel Notes and Insider Tips

Rippling River is a one-hour drive from downtown Portland and just 45 minutes from Portland International Airport. Take Highway 26 to Welches. Turn south onto Welches Road and drive one mile to the resort.

The Mount Hood area is a haven for people in love with recreation and photographers seeking nature shots. For a scenic drive around the mountain, take Highway 26 east to Highway 35 north, then turn west

on I-84. At N.E. 238th Drive, go south until you return to Highway 26. This is a day-long trip. In the summer, Mirror Mountain runs an Alpine slide ($3 per person) that speeds down Mount Hood's side for one-half mile. Stop at the Zigzag Ranger Station, two miles from Rippling River, for maps and information on miles of hiking trails. Local color flourishes in early and mid-July during Sandy Mountain Days (668-4006).

Room rates range from $69 (deluxe double) to $300 (five-bedroom condominium with maximum occupancy of ten). Winter rates are slightly lower. All prices are subject to change and are provided only for comparison.

Rippling River Resort
68010 East Fairway Avenue
Welches, OR 97067
(503) 224-7158
(800) 452-4612 (Inside Oregon)
(800) 547-8054 (Western States)

The Inn of the Seventh Mountain

Successful Northwest resorts always excel in at least one area – some boast luxurious accommodations, others championship golf, and still others gourmet food. When it comes to year-round family fun, The Inn of the Seventh Mountain sets the standards. Located within central Oregon's Deschutes National Forest, about seven miles southwest of Bend, the inn offers an expansive list of activities.

Originally, the resort's reputataion as a winter vacation spot spread on the nearby Cascade slopes. Skiers used to schussing down Mt. Bachelor began hanging their skis here in the mid-1970s. More recently, however, summer travelers have been discovering the recreational opportunities available at the inn.

Although nearly every resort features a varied list of activities, The Inn of the Seventh Mountain distinguishes itself in two special ways: First, the number of goings-on exceed that of any other resort in the region; second, the program targets every member of the family, young and old alike.

Naturally, in winter skiing sits at the top of the list – both Alpine and Nordic. Ten chairlifts access the snowy slopes of Mt. Bachelor, located 14 miles from the inn. Five-hundred acres of machine-groomed trails, ranging in difficulty from beginner to expert, offer downhill runs to skiers. In addition, fifty kilometers of marked and patrolled trails snake their way through the National Forest for those more comfortable atop skinny skis. Cross-country tours and instruction are available through the inn's recreation department. Special ski packages are also offered by the inn.

If hurtling headlong across a hilly landscape fails to capture the imagination, the inn features alternative choices. There are sleigh rides, ice skating, free arts and crafts classes, live entertainment, snowmobile tours, heated swimming pools, saunas and whirlpools.

The list goes on in summer. Included in the activities are white-water raft trips, canoe float trips, fishing trips, horseback riding, tennis programs and windsurfing. For those who prefer less structure, swimming, hiking, biking, miniature golf, volleyball, basketball and horseshoes are available. Of course, there are the saunas and whirlpools for lounging.

Twenty three-story cedar condominiums, wearing angular shake roofs sprouting smoke stacks, surround the rambling grounds. In the distance, snow-crowned Mt. Bachelor rises above a rolling pine forest.

The 316 accommodations range from a cozy standard, to a suite with a loft bedroom, to a fireside studio. For the vacationing couple the studio combines the best elements of lodging – first-class ambiance at a reasonable price. Amenities include full electric kitchens, living rooms, fireplaces, color televisions, telephones and either balconies or decks.

Two restaurants and Baron's Poolside Deli cater to the dining needs of guests. Families on a budget will find The Poppy Seed ideal. A menu featuring hot sandwiches and inexpensive entrees treats the pocketbook kindly.

On the other hand, El Crab Catcher favors the eyes and appetite. Canted ceilings, cedar walls, linen tablecloths, candle globes, brass fans and white china create the proper mood. Dinner entrees feature seafood specialties, beef, lamb and duck. Downstairs, the Crab Catcher Lounge – with its large sunken stone fireplace, dance floor, live entertainment and free movies – welcomes after-dinner guests.

As well as leisure travelers, The Inn of the Seventh Mountain also entertains conventions and gatherings. In addition to convenient function rooms, the inn can provide audio-visual equipment, can plan activities and programs, and can schedule entertainment. Groups of 20 or more should go through convention sales for information and reservations.

This is a place where people come to have fun. But here guests can combine laughs with comfort and good food.

Travel Notes and Insider Tips

Bend is located 160 miles southeast of Portland on Highway 97. Once in Bend, drive west on Wilson Avenue. Then go north on Division Street, and west on Colorado. Next, access Century Drive, which becomes Cascade Lakes Highway. Look for the inn's sign on the right.

Even though it's tempting for guests to spend all their time at the resort, visitors should explore the Bend area. The Cascade Lakes Highway winds around Mt. Bachelor, past Three Sisters and between several pristine mountain lakes. The leisurely drive offers scenic views and photo opportunities for camera buffs. After making the loop, return to Bend on Highway 97. Eleven miles south of Bend, stop at Lava Lands Visitor Center: See Lava Butte (a volcanic cone) and Lava River Caves (a lava tube nearly a mile long). Before returning to the inn, stop at Pilot Butte, located at the edge of Bend, for excellent views of the Cascades.

Lodging rates vary dramatically, with a number of special packages offered. Generally, however, summer doubles run from $42 to $180; winter prices from $46 to $212. Dinner entrees at El Crab Catcher begin at $10.95. All prices are subject to change and are provided only for comparison.

The Inn of the Seventh Mountain
P.O. Box 1207
Bend, OR 97709
(503) 382-8711
(800) 452-6810 (Inside Oregon)
(800) 547-5668 (Western States)

Washington

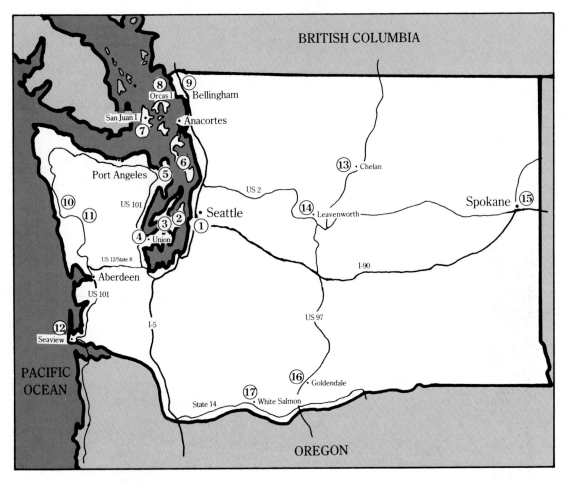

1. Alexis
   Four Seasons Olympic
   Inn at the Market
   Mayflower Park Hotel
   The Sorrento Hotel
2. The Bombay House
   Krestine
3. The Manor Farm Inn
4. Alderbrook Inn Resort
5. The Resort at Port Ludlow
6. Guest House
7. Roche Harbor Resort

8. Rosario Resort
9. Sudden Valley Resort
10. Kalaloch Lodge
11. Lake Quinault Lodge
12. The Shelburne Inn
13. Campbell's Lodge
    Whaley Mansion
14. Mountain Home Lodge
15. Cavanaugh's Inn at the Park
16. Three Creeks Lodge
17. Inn of the White Salmon

For more information about Washington, write or call:

**Washington State Department of Commerce
and Economic Development
Tourism Development Division
101 General Administration Building, AX-13
Olympia, WA 98504-0613
(800) 562-4570 (Inside Washington)
(800) 541-9274 (Outside Washington)**

Wenatchee River, Washington

Friday Harbor, San Juan Island, Washington

Stonehenge at Maryhill, Washington

Cascade Mountains, Washington

San Juan Islands, Washington

The Shelburne Inn

In some ways country inns resemble old shoes – they can be incredibly comfortable but sometimes just a little thin. Yet for people who prefer friendly old-fashioned homeyness and hospitality the "old-shoe country comfort" of inns is paradise. For these travelers The Shelburne Inn in Seaview is a great place to stay.

Located at the gateway to the Long Beach Peninsula – a 28-mile-long finger of sleepy villages, lush forests, tidewater marshes and sandy beaches – The Shelburne has been welcoming guests since 1896. In the early days wealthy Oregonians steamed into the Port of Ilwaco and then clicketyclacked up the peninsula by narrow-gauge railway. Seaview buzzed with visitors and The Shelburne hummed with excitement.

Today, following years of decline, the inn (under the guidance of current owners David Campiche and Laurie Anderson) once again thrives on a reputation of hospitality and charm. Now, however, automobiles instead of steamers deliver visitors from cities near and far.

Since those early days tourists' tastes have changed. Today's modern travelers often judge accommodations by the number of movie channels received and the locations of bathrooms. Yet The Shelburne shuns televisions and only three of its thirteen rooms feature private bathrooms. In addition, the old inn (listed on the National Register of Historic Places) has thin walls and a highway location.

Consequently, the inn is not meant for everyone, and that is a blessing! It's already nearly impossible to get a summer weekend reservation without booking weeks in advance, and even midweek vacancies can prove scarce. Travelers from near and far, searching for ambiance, personality, service and arguably the best food in the West, make The Shelburne Inn one of this region's most popular getaways.

A white picket fence fronts the green and white inn, which is actually two separate buildings bridged by a passageway. Art Nouveau floral-patterned stained glass, dating from the late 1800s and rescued from an old church in Morcambe, England, bathes the structure in reverence.

The lobby, like the entire inn, oozes turn-of-the-century charm: An open-beam ceiling strung with brass chandeliers; tongue-and-groove narrow fir paneling; a red overstuffed davenport aside a fainting couch; and a big brick fireplace paint a peaceful portrait.

Winding staircases lead to the second and third floor guest rooms that pose off a maze of hallways. Each room is different in size and color but similarly furnished – antiques and porcelain dominate. Every guest discovers Dilettante chocolates and designer toiletries waiting in the rooms.

While the inn earns high marks, it is the restaurant that garners rave reviews from critics throughout North America. Owners Tony and Ann Kischner offer a remarkable Northwest regional cuisine that reflects the availability of fresh local seasonal foods. Fifty percent of the menu changes every six weeks.

The restaurant's ambiance mirrors the theme of the inn – fir paneling, antique furniture, brass chandeliers and lace curtains garnish the surroundings. Nevertheless, it is the cuisine that tantalizes guests. Entrees range from baked filet of Pacific halibut stuffed with Dungeness crab, to homemade fettucine Creole, to the famous and popular pecan-coated sautéed chicken breast with a Dijon mustard and sour cream sauce. All breads, pastries and desserts are made on the premises.

In addition to consistently good, often exciting, food and a lengthy wine list of superior selections, the service is impeccable. Tony dances from table to table making sure of that.

The Shelburne Inn is an oasis of serenity surrounded by the drifting sands of modernism. It is a place of harmony and congeniality and one that promises dining excellence.

Travel Notes and Insider Tips

From Seattle take I-5 south to Olympia and exit Highway 101. Then take Highway 8 and 12 to Aberdeen. From there follow Highway 101 south to Seaview. From Portland take I-5 north to Kelso, then west on Highway 4 to south on Highway 101. In Seaview go north on State 103 for just a short distance; the inn is on the left.

Seaview is typical of small coastal communities: Summers bustle to the beat of tourists and winters lull to the hush of Pacific winds. The beach is a short walk from the inn through neighborhoods and across dunes. Surf fishing, beachcombing and clamming are popular. Beach driving is permitted, but watch out for pets and people. Remember, soft sand swallows tires and salt eats cars. Visit and explore Fort Canby State Park, the Lewis & Clark Interpretive Center (call 642-3029 for hours) and the north jetty viewpoint, all south of Ilwaco. Ilwaco is known as the "salmon capital of the world." For charter information, call 642-3734. For great pies visit My Mom's Pie Kitchen just north of the inn. Leadbetter Point State Park, at the tip of the peninsula, is a world of marshes and dunes sheltering hundreds of species of birds as well as deer, bear, elk and beaver. Take 103 to Joe Johns Road. In Oysterville take Oysterville Road a short distance and look for the park's sign. The road to the Point is rocky and dusty. Before leaving the peninsula, be sure to sample Willapa Bay oysters. (The Shelburne Restaurant serves them both as an appetizer and as an entree.)

Doubles, which include a large country breakfast, range from $56 to $72. Dinner entrees run from $10.75 to $16.75. All prices are subject to change and are provided only for comparison.

The Shelburne Inn
P.O. Box 250
Seaview, WA 98644
(206) 642-2442 (Hotel)
(206) 642-4142 (Restaurant)

Alderbrook Inn Resort

Alderbrook reflects the simple life. The hands of time move slowly here and airs of elegance vacation elsewhere. In many ways Alderbrook mirrors its bucolic environment.

The inn boasts a waterside location in the valley of Hood Canal's thumb. It rests within pastoral surroundings along a byway some miles from urban sprawl. This creates a vacation climate similar to owning a summer home on a private lake.

Throughout the grounds the air is charged with the distant flavor of the sea, which comes floating down the canal as it cuts a narrow swath through rolling forests of fir. In the distance, the jagged snowcapped peaks of the Olympic Mountains rise above beach bungalows dotting the shores.

Accommodations here come in two styles – modest and rustic. The true essence of this tiny Northwest corner lies within its rustic charms – the cottages. Twenty clapboard cabins, sporting moss-covered red tile roofs, form a semicircle around a sandy volleyball court. A lawn flecked with red picnic tables and tall evergreens completes the scene.

Although all of Alderbrook's buildings stand close to one another, the cottages manage to present a sense of privacy. In addition, they offer water views. The best units are 101 and 102, which sit on the waterfront. Each cottage features similar amenities – two bedrooms, a living room, a fireplace, a cozy bathroom with a shower, a kitchen and a porch. Furniture borders on used and abused, but its "broken-in" comfort is one of the benefits here.

Alderbrook's other accommodations surround a courtyard flourishing with rhododendrons, azaleas, ferns and evergreens. The three-story motel-like Lanai Building caters to guests' simplest needs. Nevertheless, the rooms are large, each has loads of drawer and shelf space, all have views and the price is right. The Plaza Building upgrades appointments to some degree and offers two suites as well. Unfortunately, some rooms are missing views.

Primarily, leisure guests come here to get away and to relax. Along similar lines, business people find the environment conducive to good work habits, while pleasant surroundings boost morale.

Leisure amenities include a 55-foot indoor swimming pool, a twin therapy pool, two saunas, an 18-hole PGA golf course, four tennis courts, a 1,200-foot dock for boating and fishing, a 600-foot beach, a volleyball court and a playground for the kids. Local tours and art workshops can be arranged.

Dining in the Beachside Room is a double delight. All tables offer refreshing views and the food is good. Entrees range from the spicy avocado supreme (avocado stuffed with crabmeat salad), to the savory crab and shrimp en casserole, to the very popular land and sea.

Alderbrook doesn't rank as the fanciest resort in the Northwest, but it is one of the most relaxing. Travelers who thrive on simplicity should enjoy their stay.

Travel Notes and Insider Tips

From Seattle take I-5 south to Olympia, then exit Highway 101 north. Drive about 35 miles to State 106 and follow it seven miles to the inn. From Portland travelers can take I-5 north to Olympia, then exit Highway 101 for the inn. Both Lake Union Air (284-2784) and the Spirit of Alderbrook (623-1445) serve Alderbrook by air and sea, respectively, from Seattle.

Conventions and groups are welcome. A number of function rooms cater to various needs and styles. The staff is well-trained and eager to serve. Plans should be made at least six months in advance. Recreation opportunities abound nearby. Four waterside state parks are within 15 miles of the resort. The Olympic National Park is just 30 miles away, as well. There are also several gift shops nearby for those who enjoy shopping.

Doubles range from $63 to $125; cottages are $80 and $90. Entrees run from $7.25 to $17.50. All prices are subject to change and are provided only for comparison.

Alderbrook Inn Resort
Highway 106
Union, WA 98592
(206) 898-2200
(206) 622-2404 (From Seattle)
(206) 621-1119 (Group Sales)

Lake Quinault Lodge

The Quinault Valley draws its lifeblood from the heavens in great gulps. Torrents of rain, curtains of fog and oceans of sun lay their nurturing sustenance upon the land. In return, the fertile floor raises tributes to nature's blessings – stately spruce, fir and cedar rise toward the skies; colorful rhododendron, huckleberry and salal form an emerald shroud; and flourishing fern, moss and lichen carpet the earth.

Within this glen's midst pose the deep blue waters of Lake Quinault, surrounded by rolling blue mountains and a verdant rain forest. This land so inspired President Franklin Delano Roosevelt that in 1938 he created the Olympic National Park. But long before F.D.R.'s visit, the Quinault Indians savored the valley's nectar. They fished trout from its lakes and streams and hunted elk in its thick woods.

By the 1880s white homesteaders trekked across the Olympics and canoed up the Quinault River to settle here. Before long a two-story log hotel stood on Lake Quinault's south shore. However, in 1922 fire swept through the building, leaving only a pile of ashes smoldering in the aftermath.

Undaunted and realizing the lake's allure, an enterprising duo, Frank McNeil, a linotype operator for the Seattle Post-Intelligencer, and Ralph Emerson, a wealthy lumberman and mill operator, joined hands. Together they received a special permit from the U.S. Forest Service, proprietors of the land, to build and operate a lodge on the site of the burned-out hotel. Working 24 hours a day and hauling building supplies over 50 miles of dirt road, a crew of laborers and craftsmen completed construction of the lodge in ten weeks. Today these efforts represent one of Washington's most popular getaways – Lake Quinault Lodge.

Located in the heart of the Olympic Peninsula, the two-story lodge looks much as it did six decades ago. Clad in brown shingles, garnished with green shutters and capped with a steep-pitched black roof, it perches atop a manicured sea of grass that descends gently to a pebbly beach trimming the lake.

A massive-beamed open ceiling, stenciled in an Indian motif, crowns the lobby. Wicker furniture, dating back to the days of McNeil and Emerson, nestles guests reading books, writing letters or simply basking in the warmth radiating from the large brick fireplace. Brass floor lamps sidle up to potted palms and Indian artifacts fill antique glass cases. Two parakeets in a gilded cage serenade; natural light washes through banks of windows. Lilacs and honeysuckle sweeten the air.

The lodge's country ambiance continues with its 30 upstairs guest rooms. Each mirrors the charm, character and personality of the structure's past: Brass or white iron beds, tiny steam radiators, hardwood floors and delicate floral-print wallpaper make up variations on a theme. There are some drawbacks – a few of the rooms share hall baths and a number of accommodations come without lake views.

In addition to accommodations in the lodge, newer Fireplace Units adjoin the older structure. They offer contemporary decor and convenience. Each of the 16 motel-like rooms boasts a gas fireplace, queen-size bed, queen sofa-bed, wall-to-wall carpeting and a cozy sitting area that rubs shoulders with a sliding glass door leading to a private deck. Each room has a view of the lake. The Lakeside Inn, built in 1923 as a temporary hotel until the lodge could be built, adds an additional eight guest rooms, bringing the total to 54. These rooms offer both privacy and rusticity.

Lake Quinault's restaurant, located in the lodge, looks out on the lake and rolling hillside. It features a Northwest cuisine highlighting seafood. The lodge's lounge is just for fun. Hunting trophies decked out in T-shirts and soft hats and an array of logging artifacts adorn the walls.

The atmosphere here breathes relaxation. There are no radios, televisions or clocks in sight; newspapers usually bear yesterday's headlines. The lobby and yard whisper tales of guests shedding tension. However,

when visitors weary of doing nothing, the lodge beckons with a long list of activities: swimming in the indoor pool, luxuriating in the Jacuzzi, sweating in the sauna or boating on the lake. There is also a recreation room with table tennis, pool tables and electronic games.

Lake Quinault Lodge, resplendent amongst towering evergreens, rolling hills and pristine waters, echoes the Northwest. It calls from its forest hideaway like gentle breezes rustling the treetops.

Travel Notes and Insider Tips

From Seattle take I-5 south to Olympia, then access Highway 101 north in Aberdeen via State 8 and U.S. 12. From Portland take I-5 north to Olympia. Travelers driving north from Portland may also choose a more scenic route by exiting State 4 west in Kelso, then taking Highway 101 north. Once in Aberdeen-Hoquiam, drive 40 miles north to the Lake Quinault South Shore Recreation Area exit. Follow the road about two miles to the lodge.

As well as activities at the lodge, hiking and fishing are popular. The Quinault Loop Trail, which starts at the lodge, is an easy hike and offers a good glimpse into the surrounding rain forest. Cutthroat, rainbow and Dolly Varden challenge anglers, but first a special license, available nearby, must be obtained from the Quinault Indians. Canoes and rowboats are available from the lodge for a small fee. Driving tours are a must. Be sure to take South Shore Road 18 miles to Graves Creek for spectacular views.

Any place this good is also extremely popular and populated, not only by couples and families but also by conventioneers taking advantage of the lodge's spacious function rooms. Therefore, weekend reservations should be made six to eight weeks in advance; plan six months to a year ahead for holiday visits. For a truly quiet getaway visit midweek during the off-season. Rains and cool weather are both distinct possibilities year-round, so come prepared.

Double rates range from $46 (Lakeside Inn) to $70 (Fireplace Unit) from June through September and slightly less the remaining months. Food is moderately priced. All rates are subject to change and are provided only for comparison.

Lake Quinault Lodge
P.O. Box 7
Quinault, WA 98575
(206) 288-2571
(800) 562-6672 (Inside Washington)

Kalaloch Lodge

Unlike Oregon's beaches, which pose seductively along Highway 101, Washington's coastline shies away from attention. It hides below tree-lined bluffs and beyond forests of fir. Except for Washington's Long Beach Peninsula and short stretches of byways tucked between Tokeland and Moclips, the ocean turns a cold shoulder to tourists here.

This is particularly true of the Olympic Peninsula, where only 15 miles of U.S. 101 offer peeks of the Pacific. To the north and south of this short corridor, which runs from Queets to just below the Hoh River and makes up the nose of Olympic National Park, Indians lay claim to all ocean-front property. Therefore, commercial activity along the western edge of the peninsula is but a dream of speculators and entrepreneurs. It is this isolation, above all else, that makes Kalaloch Lodge such a popular getaway.

Built in the late '20s and early '30s by Charles Becker and called Becker Ocean Resort, the lodge made up but one bead of a string of resorts alongside the highway. However, over the years Becker's original lodge succumbed to fire and most of the other resorts surrendered to government takeover.

Nevertheless, Becker rebuilt and became the National Park Service's first concessionaire in this area. In 1978 Marge and Larry Lesley purchased the lease and slowly began expanding and making improvements.

Twenty-one log cabins have been built since 1981. Each facility accommodates four people and features a bedroom boasting a brass bed, a cozy living room featuring a double hide-a-bed and a Franklin stove, a private bathroom and a modern kitchenette. These buildings form a semicircular pattern alongside a dozen older shake cabins that perch atop a bluff and offer the best ocean views. The cabins are private and rustic. The only drawback to the cabins is that travelers must bring their own cooking and eating utensils, as none are provided.

In addition to the cabins, Sea Crest House, a modern two-story motel nestled amongst wind-swept trees, offers 10 guest rooms. Four units have fireplaces (401, 405, 406 and 410), while all feature large picture windows that look out through the trees to the ocean.

Finally, the lodge has eight simple upstairs rooms. Only four (1, 6, 7 and 8) peer out across the Pacific; the others gaze across the highway to forested hills.

No one goes to Kalaloch to be coddled by luxurious accommodations. It is the location that draws guests by the thousands.

The resort sits on a promontory overlooking Kalaloch Creek as it flows into the ocean. Sun-bleached, surf-battered logs strew the brown sandy beach as it wraps around the bluff. Wave after wave of water foams to shore. In summer clouds of mist rise from the baking sand. The atmosphere hangs heavy with smoke curling from cabin chimneys and salted air riding the wings of ocean wind currents. Atop the bluff sit red picnic tables sidling a split-rail fence. In winter Pacific storms shower the entire scene with pelting rain and heavy wind.

This patch of ocean-front property reflects only itself: It stands alone on the Northwest Coast. Unlike its southern cousins, commercialism seems a long way from Kalaloch.

Travel Notes and Insider Tips

From Vancouver take I-5 south to State 20 west, then south to the Keystone Ferry on Whidbey Island. Once in Port Townsend, take 20 to Highway 101 north. Kalaloch lies 90 miles southwest of Port Angeles. From Seattle or Portland take I-5 to Olympia, then drive west on State 8 and U.S. 12 to Aberdeen. Kalaloch is 70 miles north alongside Highway 101.

The beach provides most of the entertainment here – clamming, beachcombing, jogging, walking and relaxing. Fishermen will find many nearby streams teeming with steelhead and in summer may also want to try dipping for ocean-run smelt. The Hoh rain forest sprawls less than an hour's drive away, while Queets is even closer. Hiking and mountain climbing are both popular within the park. The lodge's dining room serves three meals daily – seafood headlines the fare. A grocery store next to the lodge meets home-making needs. Cooking is permitted only in the cabins. Pets are allowed to stay in the cabins for an additional fee.

Doubles range in price from $38 (lodge) to $78 (fireplace cabin) in the summer. Off-season (October to June 10, Sunday through Thursday) rates are lower. Off-season rates do not apply during weekends, holidays or school vacation periods. Two-night minimum stays apply on weekends. Reservations should be made several months in advance. Dinner entrees range from $6.95 to $13.95. All prices are subject to change and are provided only for comparison.

Kalaloch Lodge
Star Route 1, Box 1100
Kalaloch, WA 98331
(206) 962-2271

The Resort at Port Ludlow

A morning mist shrouds the waters, while a solitary cormorant floats lazily on the stillness, emulating a surfer waiting for just the right wave. In the distance, the rambling shore of Whidbey Island rises to touch the horizon as it expands to conquer the night. Charcoal gray smoke from a steaming freighter curls just beneath the awakening skies.

So begins another morning at Port Ludlow, a thumb of land just north of the Hood Canal. The view from the natural wood condominiums presents a picture of water and rolling shorelines. It's a world of blues and greens.

As the sun rises in the sky and the mist burns off, the clamor of vacationers replaces the hush of nature. Horseshoes clank against sunken stakes, voices echo from the grassy volleyball court and kids navigating yellow paddle boats splash across the saltwater lagoon. Despite the activities, peace and relaxation pose just seconds away: Guests relax in their rentals, sail peacefully across the bay and shoot rounds of golf.

Whether it's working up a sweat or whiling away the hours, Port Ludlow offers a full range of activities. However, boating and golfing head the list.

Boaters can appreciate both the location and the facilities. The resort sits on the edge of Port Ludlow Bay, a sheltered deep-water harbor, and boasts a 300-slip marina, with slips ranging in length from 24 to 50 feet. In addition, local operators offer both bareboat charters and skippered cruises.

To Washington golfers, golf and Port Ludlow have come to mean the same thing. The American Society of Golf Course Architects ranks the resort's 18-hole championship course, designed by Robert Muir Graves, in the nation's top one percent. It's a sea of green as it rolls and meanders through a forest of fir. Each hole has been hewed out of the woods and is a solitary oasis. Only the whirr of golf carts and the songs of birds break the stillness.

Of course there are other activities, including a summer recreation program for children. Also featured are an outdoor swimming pool, indoor heated lap pool, a Jacuzzi, two saunas, seven plex-a-pave tennis courts, hiking trails, bicycling paths, a squash court and a recreation room.

The condominiums nestle on a tree-lined slope that gradually descends toward the water. Their distance from the main lodge, marina and beach club permits easy access but also allows for privacy and tranquillity. Each

unit is privately owned and therefore features an individual style of decor. They range in size from apartments with lofts to deluxe bedrooms. All accommodations have private baths, telephones and televisions. The apartments come with living rooms, fully equipped kitchens, dining rooms, fireplaces, private decks and water views. No matter what type of unit guests choose, however, they should always seek an accommodation with a water view in order to fully appreciate the beauty of the surroundings.

Diners congregate at the Harbormaster Restaurant, which looks out over a forest of bobbing masts to the snow-capped Olympics in the distance. Flickering brass lamps adorn aqua linen tablecloths; rough-hewn posts support a cathedral ceiling. Dinner entrees range from bacon-wrapped filet mignon to poulet Dungeness. The fare is moderately good, while the wine list is small but adequate.

The Resort at Port Ludlow was planned in 1967 by the Pope and Talbot Lumber Company. Like John Gray, Salishan's developer, the company envisioned a resort that plays in concert with its surroundings. As a result, the resort melds perfectly with its environment.

Travel Notes and Insider Tips

From Seattle take the Winslow Ferry, then take State 305. Go north on State 3 to the Hood Canal Bridge. Cross the bridge, take the first right onto Paradise Bay Road and follow it to the resort. From Vancouver take I-5 south to Whidbey Island via State 20. Once on the island take the Keystone Ferry to Port Townsend. Here, pick up State 20 again and follow the signs to Port Ludlow. From Portland take I-5 north to Olympia, then take Highway 101 north through Shelton toward Port Townsend. Nine miles north of Quilcene take State 104 toward the Hood Canal Bridge. Just before reaching the bridge take a left on Paradise Bay Road and follow it to Port Ludlow. NOTE: Paradise Bay Road is not well marked.

As well as caring for leisure travelers, Port Ludlow caters to groups and conventions. For more information call the resort and ask for the group sales office. Sightseers and history buffs will delight in the resort's location. Port Gamble, an old but still active mill town, sits just across the Hood Canal Bridge. The town resembles a New England village. Be sure to visit the museum and the general store. The Scandinavian village of Poulsbo lies south of Port Gamble. It is a good spot for gift shopping and for those with a sweet tooth. The town celebrates Viking Fest in mid-May and its Scandinavian Midsommer Festival in mid-June. To the west of Port Ludlow is the historic community of Port Townsend, blessed with an array of Victorian homes and remarkably good music festivals. (Call Centrum, 385-3102, for a schedule.) Majestic Hurricane Ridge rises about an hour's drive away, just outside of Port Angeles. Good hiking and great views are available. Finally, Seattle is less than 90 minutes away, and Victoria can be easily accessed from Port Angeles via the ferry.

From May 1 to October 15 rates run from $89 for a deluxe bedroom (no view), while apartments begin at $126. Off-season rates are considerably less. Dinner entrees range from $12.75 to $16.75. All prices are subject to change and are provided only for comparison.

The Resort at Port Ludlow
781 Walker Way
Port Ludlow, WA 98365
(206) 437-2222
(800) 732-1239 (Inside Washington)

The Manor Farm Inn

The Manor Farm Inn combines a little bit of magic with a large dose of country. It is Dorothy walking down the yellow brick road to James Herriot's Yorkshire and Alice discovering that Wonderland is a 30-acre farm tucked into the verdant hillsides of the Kitsap Peninsula.

Most of all, the inn is a world of natural wonders, pastoral simplicity and scenic serenity. It is a place where pampering and coddling represent the nature of things, and the concrete idols shadowing ambition and anxiety spawn distant worlds away. It is a getaway made for dreaming created by a dreamer.

Manor Farm Inn poses like a French country farmhouse set back from Big Valley Road, a winding, narrow stretch of blacktop that occasionally guides an automobile past a few sprawling farms. White rail fences contain the inn's gentle farmlands; a long gravel driveway prevents their formal introduction. On one side, the sheep bury their black faces into the grasses; on the other, plump Jerseys and frisky horses share a scrumptious repast. Ducks, chickens, turkeys, geese, pheasants and guinea hens flap around and about. Flower beds burst everywhere in a kaleidoscopic celebration, while yellow roses climb and cling to the rails and banisters of a covered veranda.

Guests arrive (never more than 22 total) to the greetings of Manor Farm's resident dreamer, the energetic Robin Hughes. He cuts the figure of a handsome Englishman, smiling with sparkling blue eyes, dashing about with joy in every step and constantly reflecting on future plans to nurture his guests. He presents a marvelous, though slightly disheveled, appearance. He is Manor Farm's guru – the person who cares for his guests and meets their every need so they can relax and smell the roses, because, above all else, this is a place to get in touch with repressed passions.

"We have creature comforts here," Robin explains, "good food, bright and cheerful rooms, excellent amenities and lots of things to do. But I want people to get into feelings and emotions, not what's here for facilities."

And that's what Manor Farm Inn is all about. It's a retreat – a piece of Utopia, where guests say hello to nature, read the great works, fish for trout, soak in the hot tub, sip fine wine, savor gourmet food and make acquaintance with life.

Travel Notes and Insider Tips

From Seattle take the ferry to Winslow. Follow State 305 through Poulsbo to Highway 3, then drive north to Big Valley Road. Turn right and drive 1.5 miles to the inn. The entire trip takes about an hour.

The guest rooms are both comfortable and elegant. They feature French country pine antiques; down comforters; vaulted ceilings; private bathrooms; fresh flowers; gifts of chocolates, nut breads and tea cakes; and views of rolling farmland. Two suites have fireplaces. Dining is meant to be an experience lasting several hours and is open to both inn guests and the general public. The traditional dining fare is a set five-course dinner, offered at a fixed price and served at a set time. In addition, there is an adjacent dining room where diners may order "a la carte" from the fixed menu, which changes on a nightly basis. For overnight guests, a full breakfast is included in the room rates. Activities include fly fishing in the inn's trout pond, bicycling country lanes, golfing at nearby Port Ludlow, sightseeing (Seattle, Winslow, Poulsbo and Port Gamble head the list) and communicating with nature. The inn also features unique monthly events ranging from Scottish Highland games in May, to a country hoedown in June, to Christmas feasts in December.

Doubles range from $55 to $85. The five-course dinner costs $30 per person. Children and pets are not accepted, and smoking is not permitted in any of the rooms. All prices are subject to change and are provided only for comparison.

The Manor Farm Inn
26069 Big Valley Road N.E.
Poulsbo, WA 98370
(206) 779-4628

Seattle

Like its smaller sister city to the south, Seattle has always boasted of its livability, its commitment to people, parks and open spaces. While this attitude contributed to the "good life," it also promoted cautious growth and expansion, which ultimately translated into provincialism. As a result, Seattle gained a reputation for inspiring a laid-back lifestyle amidst mountains, lakes and an inland sea. Although this environment proved great for residents who loved the quiet life, it spelled boredom to those people – residents and travelers alike – seeking an urban experience.

Today, however, Seattle is a city in transition: A new skyline rises toward the heavens. In the streets below, a busy financial district and a trendy shopping center bustle with human activity.

This new spirit began its evolution in 1962, when Seattle hosted the Century 21 World's Fair. Visitors by the thousands came; some returned to make Seattle their home. This influx of tourists and new residents breathed new life into the city. It also encouraged the long-time residents and the power brokers to consider melding the best of both worlds – country and city.

As a result, a vibrancy has arisen around the spirit of two landmarks – one representing the old, the other conjuring up the future.

The first, Pike Place Market, reigns as the nation's oldest continuously operating farmers' market. It is also Seattle's soul. Here, amongst seven acres of mix-and-match architecture, a hodgepodge of the city's people meet to shop and browse amidst a gantlet of stalls and a bevy of shops and restaurants.

The second, Seattle Center, still draws more tourists than any downtown site. In fact, the venerable Space Needle continues to rank as Seattle's number two tourist attraction, right behind the Washington State Ferries. Unlike other cities, Seattle's legacy to a World's Fair has turned out to be more than just another parking lot.

However, neither of these sites touch upon Seattle's sophisticated side as it appears in the '80s. The city's cosmopolitan face freshens up along and beside fashionable Fifth Avenue. Here residents and visitors alike happily part with their money at such quality department stores as The Bon and Frederick & Nelson and such chic boutiques as Jaeger's and Totally Michael's in Rainier Square.

Seattle's other downtown personalities thrive on the city's south side. The International District and Pioneer Square, each located within a block of the Kingdome, both beckon visitors, but for very different reasons. The District boasts an array of Asian markets and restaurants, while the Square is a haven for art galleries and unusual shops.

Despite the sprouting of glass and steel, Seattle's heart still beats within its people. Where better to check a city's pulse than within its neighborhoods? In Seattle that means a visit to Capitol Hill – home to the city's bohemian side – and Queen Anne – a mirror reflecting Seattle's cross section.

Renovation and revitalization have brought a new cosmopolitan verve to Seattle. Yet the development hasn't meant a decline in the city's livability. Now Seattle is both a good place to visit and a great place to live.

Travel Notes and Insider Tips

Interstate 5 cuts a wide swath through the city's heart, while Seattle-Tacoma International Airport is a 25-minute drive from downtown. Visitors should leave their cars parked for the duration of their stay and become familiar with the Metro (447-4800) bus drivers.

Seattle's best food can be found at Labuznik (1924 First Avenue, 682-1624) and The Other Place (319 Union, 623-7340). Be sure to visit the following: Seattle Art Museum (447-4710), Museum of History and Industry (324-1125), Elliott Bay Book Company (a Seattle landmark and haunt, with a great selection of books and beverages, 624-6600) and Uwajimaya (a Japanese department and grocery store, 624-6248). For fun and wonderful views take the 30-minute ferry ride (walk on) to Winslow and Bainbridge Island.

For more information about Seattle write or call: Seattle-King County Convention & Visitors Bureau, 1815 Seventh Avenue, Seattle, WA 98101 (447-4240). All of the above numbers are in area code 206.

The Sorrento Hotel

As they are checking out, the young bride and her still-nervous husband thank the desk clerk, telling him that everything was perfect. Then the bell captain lifts their baggage and the just-marrieds turn to leave. But before they reach the door, the clerk turns their heads with one final message: "By the way," he says, "I hope you don't mind, but we took the liberty of washing your car and vacuuming the rice." The couple nod in astonishment and stroll hand-in-hand to their shiny automobile.

This represents a nice touch, but for regular guests of the Sorrento the personal care and service that deeds such as this represent come as no surprise. It is precisely this coddling aspect that has revived the Sorrento and other similar small luxury hotels throughout the region. And it is this attitude of service that once again makes these hotels the popular choices of sophisticated corporate guests and discriminating leisure travelers.

Like so many of its renovated brethren, the Sorrento boasts a treasured past. Built in 1909 and fashioned after Italian Renaissance structures found on the Riviera, the Sorrento welcomed President Taft as its first guest and then enjoyed several decades as the toast of the town. Perched atop First Hill in a residential area, it offered spectacular city and water views amidst the trappings of luxury.

However, as Seattle's rising skyline began casting shadows across the hotel's windows, the Sorrento gradually lost its clientele to the newer and bigger hotels downtown. Then in 1980, two Seattle businessmen poured $4.5 million and large chunks of their hearts into renovating the hotel. They halved the number of rooms to 76; scrubbed the place inside and out; carved a circular drive that is bordered by a wrought-iron fence and centered by an Italian fountain; and carefully selected an enthusiastic general manager, a quality chef and a snappy staff of 90.

Today elegance, attention to detail and personal service mark the Sorrento. The rooms are tastefully appointed, melding antiques, stuffed furniture, green plants and Oriental art. In addition, there is an array of modern amenities such as color televisions; stereos;

telephones with bathroom extensions; designer toiletries; wet bars and refrigerators featuring soft drinks, Pike Place Nuts and Dilettante Chocoloates; and morning deliveries of the "Wall Street Journal."

On the ground floor pose the Hunt Club Room, the hotel's fine restaurant and lounge, and the Fireside Room, the Sorrento's warm lobby. Fresh regional seafood – served within intimate surroundings of mahogany, brick and open beams – highlights the restaurant's fare. Polished Honduras mahogany, an emerald Rookwood fireplace and a grand piano set off the lobby.

The Sorrento Hotel rekindles the spirit of the past, while catering to the needs of the present. It is place where service is more than a line on a brochure.

Travel Notes and Insider Tips

Travelers heading south on I-5 should take the Columbia-James exit, then travel east on Cherry. Turn left at Terry, then drive several blocks to Madison and the Sorrento's circular drive for valet parking. North-bounders can simply take the Madison-James exit to a right on Madison. The Seattle-Tacoma International Airport is about a 25-minute drive south of the hotel.

The hotel's location represents both a plus and a minus. On the plus side, its residential environment is quieter than places in the city's heart; on the minus side, it is a healthy walk to Seattle's business community. Meeting facilities here are not aimed at conventioneers. Basically, there are two small function rooms and the Penthouse Executive Suite. For city views and peeks at the bay, guests must be above the third floor. There is no concierge; however, the front desk can arrange for everything from limousine service to theater tickets. Before leaving the Sorrento for a return trip home, investigate nearby Capitol Hill. Be sure to walk and shop Broadway between Denny and Mercer and also to visit the Seattle Art Museum, the conservatory and the top of the water tower in Volunteer Park.

Doubles run from $105 to $120 for a deluxe, $135 to $155 for suites and $250 to $625 for penthouse suites. Weekend rates are considerably less, and group rates are available upon request. Complete dinners for two will cost about $75. All prices are subject to change and are provided only for comparison.

The Sorrento Hotel
900 Madison Street
Seattle, WA 98104
(206) 622-6400
(800) 426-1265 (Outside Washington)

Inn at the Market

The hands on the big clock atop the Main Arcade mark the passing of time, while below, cars crawl around the bend of bricked Pike Place, carefully weaving their way through throngs of shoppers. Under the Arcade's flat roof, fish vendors hawk their shiny catch, butchers trim the fat off tender fillets and farmers keep their stalls piled high with kaleidoscopic mosaics of fruits and vegetables.

The air is filled with the smells of salmon commingling with the salty sea and the sounds of shoppers, buskers and peddlers singing a cacophony of consumerism. Throughout Pike Place Market, a seven-acre inner-city neighborhood, Seattle's heart pulses with excitement. The Arcade's stalls and the Market's specialty shops, French bakeries and ethnic restaurants buzz with Seattle's people and the world's travelers.

Located one block from the Main Arcade and making up part of the Market's border sits the Inn at the Market. Like the Market itself – a collection of mix-and-match architecture and a hodgepodge of humanity – the inn defies categorization.

Originally, the Inn at the Market billed itself as a bed-and-breakfast inn, which it isn't. More recently, it has gone to calling itself a small hotel, a more accurate description. However, its size – 65 rooms – and its ambiance – country elegance – really make it resemble more of what its name suggests – a city inn.

The inn's brick-and-concrete facade, accented by bay windows, wraps around a brick courtyard. Restaurants and shops embrace a bubbling fountain, potted plants and a 50-year-old cherry tree. Off the courtyard sits the inn's lobby, a homey environment of overstuffed furniture, country antiques and a brick fireplace.

Many of the upstairs rooms offer views of the bay. All are bright and cheery, with amenities such as refrigerators, coffee makers, windows that open, telephones with bathroom extensions and color televisions. The decor is country pine and plush comfort.

With the 1985 opening of the Inn at the Market, Seattle's accommodations came full circle. Every taste and need can now be catered to. For travelers wishing to combine an inner-city experience with a Northwest flair, the Inn at the Market should be given first consideration.

Travel Notes and Insider Tips

From I-5, north-bounders should exit Seneca Street and continue west to First Avenue. Then go four blocks north to Pine Street and take a left to the inn. South-bounders should exit Stewart Street to First Avenue, then take a left one block to Pine Street. Seattle-Tacoma International Airport is a 25-minute drive south of downtown.

In the Market's Main Arcade, be sure to visit DeLaurenti's, an Italian grocery store and deli; Maximilien-in-the-Market, a French restaurant with a bay view; the Athenian Inn, a taste of local color and good beer; Le Panier, one of the city's best bakeries; Il Bistro, serving a great roast rack of lamb; and the Pink Door, a funky Italian restaurant with good food. The best advice in this neighborhood is to explore on foot.

All the rooms here are spacious, with the Parlor Suites being the best buys. If you want water views, ask for a room on the Post Alley side of the inn. Doubles begin at $78 for rooms and $133 for suites. The inn doesn't have a restaurant. All prices are subject to change and are provided only for comparison.

Inn at the Market
86 Pine Street
Seattle, WA 98101
(206) 443-3600
(800) 446-4484 (Outside Washington)

Mayflower Park Hotel

Seattle's hotel boom has produced a golden vein of rich accommodations. Most cater to corporate executives and moneyed travelers. Within this sea of luxury, however, floats an island of moderation – the Mayflower Park Hotel. Its 200 rooms lure middle managers, leisure travelers and families who want nice rooms at moderate prices.

"This is our market," Marie Dempcy, manager and co-owner, explains. "We're giving our guests a nice place to stay at a moderate price. Frankly, we give good value."

Located downtown in the center of Seattle's department store district, the hotel dispenses more than comfort and price. It also offers convenience. The Bon, Frederick & Nelson, Nordstrom and the monorail terminal cup the 12-story hotel in their palms.

Today this downtown location translates into advantages for shoppers, leisure travelers and business people. However, before Marie arrived in 1974, this central site also contributed to the hotel's deterioration. For a number of years its guests consisted primarily of call girls and their clients. Marie kicked the girls out, then restored, redecorated and refurnished the 60-year-old building.

Now the lobby boasts traditional furniture, brass table lamps and large potted plants which create a living room ambiance. An arched glass entranceway and an Italian crystal chandelier add touches of understated elegance.

Around by the elevators, Oliver's, the hotel's bar, flashes glass and chrome, but a friendly human atmosphere balances its cold modern look. Carnations and soft colors soften the decor, while large windows look out on a busy streetscape.

At the opposite end of the lobby, a short flight of stairs leads down to Clippers, the Mayflower's award-winning restaurant. Rattan chairs, marble tabletops, brass trim and classic columns make up an elegant setting. An L-shaped dining area wraps around the lower level, creating a sense of space and privacy. Dining is a civilized experience, serene and unhurried. Breakfasts are considered to be among the best in the city, while dinner entrees, ranging from sporelli vegetali to fillet of salmon, are quite good.

The guest rooms don't equal the public areas in elegance but are comfortable and quiet. Decor tends to be contemporary and each room features a telephone and a television. Double-paned glass windows keep out street noise; air conditioning chases away summer heat.

In many ways the Mayflower Park Hotel offers the best value in town. It is certainly Seattle's best hotel for travelers whose pocketbooks have never had a weight problem.

Travel Notes and Insider Tips

North-bounders should exit I-5 at Seneca Street, then turn right on Fourth Avenue. South-bounders should exit Stewart Street, turn left on Fifth Avenue, then right on Pine Street, to a right on Fourth Avenue.

The monorail accesses The Seattle Center. At the Center, visit the Space Needle for a great view of the city, the Center House for pricey gifts and fast food, and Fun Forest for rides and laughs. The Center also hosts the Northwest Folklife Festival (625-4410) – the largest free music and dance festival in the United States – on Memorial Day weekend, and Bumbershoot (625-4275) – a festival celebrating the arts – on Labor Day weekend. As well as the department stores, shoppers should walk down fashionable Fifth Avenue and over to Pike Place Market. See page 52 for more Seattle tips.

Room doubles begin at $58 for standards and $90 for suites. Dinner entrees range from $5.50 for a light meal to $13.95 for a main course selection. All prices are subject to change and are provided only for comparison.

Mayflower Park Hotel
405 Olive Way
Seattle, WA 98101
(206) 623-8700
(800) 562-4504 (Inside Washington)
(800) 426-5100 (Outside Washington)

Alexis

The Alexis Hotel is the story of a frog turning into a prince. Its metamorphosis reflects the delivery of a neighborhood – the rebirth of a section of Seattle's downtown that had been taken over by despair and degeneration.

The tale began in 1901. That was when Max Umbrecht designed and built the four-story Globe Building. At first it housed the business activities of prominent Seattle businessman J.W. Clise. In 1917 Clise departed, marking the beginning of a 60-year decline of both the building and the neighborhood. During the '20s, tailors, pawnbrokers and proprietors of greasy spoons inhabited the Globe. Then, while the depression cut the heart out of people's souls, wrecking crews smashed the guts out of the Globe and turned it into a parking garage. For decades Umbrecht's humiliated edifice watched as First Avenue became littered with deterioration.

Finally, however, white knights charged down the waterfront avenue. Representing Paul Schell's Cornerstone Development Company, they began renovating a six-square-block area between Madison and Seneca. Called Waterfront Place, the project transformed a seedy area into a trendy neighborhood, with the Alexis rising out of the Globe's ruins to become the development's grand centerpiece.

Surrounded today by stylish boutiques, chic restaurants and modish health clubs, the 54-room Alexis ranks as Seattle's finest small luxury hotel. Service, elegance and attention to detail softly caress each and every guest.

Upon the arrival of guests, the doorman – who speaks several languages, a sign of the hotel's international flavor – welcomes them to the Alexis, handles their bags, guides them to the front desk and slips away to park their car. There is never a moment of lingering about, waiting for the deep dig into pockets that signals the customary tip. Service is performed joyously here, and tipping is neither expected nor accepted.

The lobby mirrors the hotel's subtle grandeur. A quiet, dignified ambiance emanates from the pilasters and coffered ceiling. Marble and brass commingle with rich colors and fresh flowers; antiques meld with classic plush chairs. Sun pours through a skylight, which illuminates a grand stairway climbing from the Madison Street entrance. Delicious smells waft from the restaurant, located at the top of the stairs.

This understated elegance continues in the guest rooms. Steeped in an ambiance best described as residential, the rooms are dressed in antiques and custom furniture; they are trimmed with the ubiquitous marble and brass.

The accommodations include 18 suites, three of which have fireplaces. Amenities such as built-in bars, down comforters, whirlpool baths, writing tables, telephones with bathroom extensions, designer toiletries, terry robes, contained and concealed color televisions, fresh flowers, morning newspaper delivery, complimentary sherry and complimentary continental breakfasts pamper guests.

As well as providing luxurious facilities, the Alexis features one of Seattle's best restaurants. Using fresh local ingredients prepared in a French style, the fare ranges from Whidbey Island mussels steamed with Riesling and herbs, to roast rack of lamb with chestnut and pear sauce. The intimate restaurant favors a stylish, softly lit decor.

A rising star glitters over the Alexis Hotel, while its chic supporting cast makes Waterfront Place an excellent location for Seattle's best small hotel.

Travel Notes and Insider Tips

From I-5 south-bounders should exit Columbia-James, then go a few blocks north to Madison. Follow Madison to the hotel. North-bounders should exit Seneca and follow Seneca to First Avenue, then go one block south to the Alexis. The Seattle-Tacoma International Airport is a 25-minute drive from downtown.

The Alexis is four blocks from Pike Place Market, three blocks from Pioneer Square, three blocks from the financial district and just a few

blocks from the Washington State Ferry Terminal. Besides the fruit and vegetable stalls and the fish vendors at the market, be sure to visit DeLaurenti's (an Italian grocery), The Athenian for lunch and Le Panier for dessert. In Pioneer Square don't miss the Elliott Bay Cafe and Bookstore (a popular hangout). Call 464-6400 for a ferry schedule: Rides to Bainbridge Island are a must.

Double occupancies range from $120 (guest rooms), to $140 (twin rooms and parlor suites), to $225 (executive suites), to $240 (fireplace suites). Dinner entrees range from $8.50 to $23. All prices are subject to change and are provided only for comparison.

Alexis
1007 First Avenue
Seattle, WA 98104
(206) 624-4844
(800) 426-7033 (Outside Washington)

Four Seasons Olympic

The Four Seasons Olympic holds a position of luxury unmatched in this region. While a few hotels in Seattle, Portland and Vancouver offer rooms that are every bit as elegant, travelers must venture to the world's most sophisticated cities to experience the grandeur of the Olympic. Some may find this lavishness bordering on gaudy, but no one can deny the rich atmosphere it inspires.

Located in the heart of Seattle's fashionable Fifth Avenue – a microcosm of its New York namesake – the service begins before guests even enter the 450-room hotel. As visitors drive their cars up the circular drive fronting the recessed entrance, a valet and the doorman, both smartly dressed, rush to lend a hand.

Surprisingly, the grandeur of the hotel and the sophistication of much of its clientele don't translate into stuffy surroundings. In fact, the entire staff, from valet to concierge, manage to make every guest feel quite relaxed and at home, no easy task since only a palace-residence could equal this environment.

The lobby is grand in every way – rich oak-paneled walls rise from terrazzo floors; classic armchairs sit amongst lush potted plants and fragrant floral displays; crystal-draped chandeliers scintillate overhead; and marble and brass seem to be everywhere. Throughout the day well-dressed guests stroll about talking in hushed tones. In the afternoon visitors sip tea in the Garden Court Lounge. And in the evening diners savor the excellent French cuisine offered in The Georgian.

As can be expected, rooms here are pricey, bathed in good taste and feature lots of extras. Color schemes of gray, peach and light brown imbue residential furnishings and rich fabrics. Amenities include robes, twice-daily maid service, evening turn-down and chocolates, designer toiletries, bathroom telephone extensions, 24-hour room service, around-the-clock concierge service, one-hour pressing, same-day laundry and complimentary shoeshine.

In addition to the hotel's facilities, 14 nationally and internationally famous retail shops – from Abercrombie & Fitch to Gene Juarez – occupy space here. While back in the hotel, a health club features an indoor pool, whirlpool, sun deck, saunas, exercise equipment and, for the dedicated sybarite, massages by appointment.

This luxurious atmosphere lies upon a rich tradition. The original Olympic Hotel opened in 1924. Its construction was of granite and terra cotta brick, trimmed with high Palladian windows. Hundreds of antique mirrors, Italian and Spanish oil jars and bronze statuary decorated its interior. The result was a polished diamond set within a cradle of provincialism.

Today, following a $60-million restoration in 1982, the Four Seasons Olympic is as grand as ever. But its setting has changed. Now, after a decade of renovation and revitalization, Seattle is attaining a level of cosmopolitanism worthy of such a luxurious hotel.

Travel Notes and Insider Tips

From I-5 north-bounders should exit Seneca Street to downtown and the hotel. South-bounders take the Columbia-James exit to Fourth Avenue, then north to University and the hotel.

This location is right in the middle of both the financial and shopping districts. As well as the retail stores in the hotel, Rainier Square – home to 50 chic boutiques and restaurants – is located just across the street. The Bon, Frederick & Nelson, Nordstrom and I. Magnin are only four blocks north. For sightseeing, Metro bus Number 74 is the best way to travel to the International District, the Kingdome and Pioneer Square. The monorail terminal for the Seattle Center is at Fourth and Pine, alongside Nordstrom. Although the Four Seasons oozes wealth, it does cater very well to a diverse clientele. To attract families and the leisure traveler, the hotel offers special weekend rates. For business meetings, receptions, formal dinners or special occasions, the hotel's meeting rooms and catering services are the best in town.

Doubles begin at $145. The Four Seasons Room (French doors separate the conversation area from the bedroom) costs $190. Petite suites are $205, deluxe suites begin at $350. The Presidential Suite and the Governors Suite run $800. Dinner entrees in The Georgian range from $14 to $26. All prices are subject to change and are provided only for comparison.

Four Seasons Olympic
411 University Street
Seattle, WA 98101
(206) 621-1700
(800) 821-8106 (Inside Washington)
(800) 223-8772 (Outside Washington)
(800) 268-6282 (Inside Canada)

The Bombay House & Krestine

In 1985, Bob Scott and Georgene Hagen added a touch of high seas adventure to their bed-and-breakfast business when they purchased the Baltic trading ketch Krestine. Now the innkeepers can offer their island guests a choice of either land or sea.

Bainbridge Island sprawls within eyesight of downtown Seattle: It's a mere 30-minute ferry ride away. Nevertheless, this bucolic retreat hosts quiet communities of commuters and artists, who favor the isle's tree-lined hills and its isolated serenity to the concrete mountains and commercial activities of the city. It possesses the kind of country milieu which enhances the bed-and-breakfast experience.

There is little doubt that this atmosphere contributes considerably to the success of The Bombay House. Located in the former mill town of West Blakely, a sleepy unincorporated community of fewer than 50 bungalows, this three-story Victorian house commands an enchanting perch. Its sloping lawns burst with flowers, while four large evergreens shade a rough-cedar gazebo. Atop the house stands a widow's walk – its rails look out across the dark gray glassy waters of Rich Passage.

Inside, a brick fireplace crackles with warmth. The sun washes through tall windows which look out on the rooftops of town. Overstuffed furniture melds with antiques such as an 1850 square grand piano and four hand-crafted violins. Five bedrooms, two downstairs and three upstairs, also boast an antique look.

The protective arms of Eagle Harbor spread about ten minutes away. Amongst the hollow echo of Washington's ferries and the bobbing masts of sailboats floats the Krestine. It welcomed its first overnight guests, a honeymooning couple, on April 6, 1985.

The guest cabins sit within the bowels of this double-masted ship. Wooden beams run the length of its 100 feet, while inside skylights and brass hurricane lamps throw light about its 1904 hull. A wood stove removes the chill from Puget Sound; hanging plants and old photographs carry away the ship's hard lines.

Travelers to Washington often select island hideaways for their vacations. But few locations can boast such choices. On Bainbridge Island guests can have country or city, land or sea.

Travel Notes and Insider Tips

From Seattle, take the ferry to Winslow on Bainbridge Island. The Krestine is moored in the harbor; The Bombay House is several back roads away. The innkeepers will pick guests up at the dock.

Bainbridge Island is best known for relaxing, bicycling and clam digging. A good site for picnicking is Fay Bainbridge State Park. Both Winslow and nearby Poulsbo feature unique shops. On the way to Poulsbo, stop off at the Suquamish Museum, which is devoted to the history and culture of the Salish Indians. Dinner should be taken in Seattle. For tips on Seattle, see page 52.

Double rates at The Bombay House range from $45 to $68, while at the Krestine they run from $60 to $75. A continental breakfast is included at both places, and shared bathrooms are standard fare. The Krestine is cozy and warm, but visitors should remember that it is an old ship, not a modern yacht. All prices are subject to change and are provided only for comparison.

The Bombay House & Krestine
8490 N.E. Beck Road
Bainbridge Island, WA 98110
(206) 842-3926 (Bombay House)
(206) 842-5100 (Krestine)

Guest House

Guest House proves that bed-and-breakfast accommodations are as diverse as they are numerous. In fact, Guest House is unlike any other bed and breakfast in this region.

Located on 45-mile-long Whidbey Island, just 90 minutes from Seattle, Guest House sits on a rolling meadow which tucks its shoulder into an evergreen forest. Saratoga Passage and the Cascade Mountains peek through the trees which sprout from across State 525.

Each of the accommodations here is unique. The farmhouse, which was built in the 1920s, houses a traditional bed-and-breakfast guest room. It features a private entrance, bedroom, sitting room and bathroom. At 9 a.m., breakfast baskets arrive at the door steaming with homemade delicacies.

So much for tradition. Secluded at the edge of the woods sit three cottages. Hansel & Gretel is a rustic log cabin, complete with a sleeping loft. The Carriage House boasts two skylights and a large picture window, while knotty pine walls embrace an antique brass bed. The third facility, the Farm Guest Cottage, features a large deck in a sunny setting. All of the cottages include televisions, airtight fireplaces, cozy kitchens, private baths and electric heat.

The big prize at Guest House perches on the edge of a wildlife pond. Originally built as a private home, this 2,200-square-foot log lodge blends rusticity and luxury. Wrapped around a massive stone fireplace, which is bordered by walls of glass, are amenities such as air conditioning, a microwave oven, a dishwasher, a washer and dryer, wall-to-wall carpeting and a king-size bed. In addition, the lodge is furnished in antiques, has several televisions and boasts two large bathrooms.

As well as roomy and comfortable accommodations, Guest House offers extras seldom envisioned by bed-and-breakfast travelers. Besides a hot tub, which is standard fare these days, a swimming pool and a dressing room – with an exercise bike, a rowing machine and a suntan lamp – grace the grounds.

The setting here is lush and wildlife abounds: Bald eagles soar overhead, deer roam about and African geese wade in the pond. Nestled within this pristine environment, Guest House ranks as one of the area's best bed and breakfasts and certainly the most varied in accommodations and amenities.

Travel Notes and Insider Tips

Traveling south on I-5 from Vancouver, B.C., go west and south on Highway 20, which becomes State 525. Proceed one mile past Greenbank, then turn right onto Christenson Road. Take the first driveway on the right for Guest House. From Seattle, take I-5 north to exit 189, then go to the Mukilteo Ferry Dock. Once on the island, follow State 525 16 miles to Christenson Road.

Whidbey Island is an ideal getaway: It's isolated yet still near urban centers. For excellent Dungeness crabbing, take Maxwelton Road just outside of Clinton to the beach at Maxwelton. There is a picnic area and a boat ramp there as well. At the opposite end of the road sits Langley, a quaint seaside village loaded with art galleries, antique stores and arts and crafts shops. Visit the Dog House Tavern for pitchers of ale and local color. North of the Guest House, take Route 113 to Fort Casey State Park. On the grounds are bunkers, gun emplacements, a lighthouse museum, beaches and commanding bluffs. Nearby Coupeville dates back to the 1850s. History buffs should visit The John Alexander Blockhouse just off Front Street. Michael's Cafe and The Captain Whidbey boast the island's best food. Oak Harbor is the largest of Whidbey's towns: It has a golf course and a large marina. Don't fail to visit nearby Deception Pass State Park. It offers four miles of sandy beaches, hiking through 1,740 acres of virgin timber, swimming, picnicking, photo opportunities and freshwater fishing at Cranberry Lake.

Guest House does not permit smoking inside the rooms nor children under 14. Breakfast is included in the rates for the Wildflower Suite but is an additional $5 charge in the cottages and the log lodge. Doubles run from $60 for the suite, $65 for the cottages and $120 for the lodge. All prices are subject to change and are provided only for comparison.

Guest House
835 East Christenson Road
Greenbank, WA 98253
(206) 678-3115

Sudden Valley Resort

The '80s will be remembered as the decade when yuppy became our favorite acronym, World's Fairs sprouted and withered like weeds, and the Soviets boasted a younger leader than the Americans. It is also the decade of condominium resorts. Sudden Valley falls into that category.

Located at the southern end of Lake Whatcom, about four miles outside of Bellingham, the resort sprawls across 1,500 acres of lakefront, hills, forests and meadows. Rising from the lake, the rolling Chuckanut Mountains overlook natural wood condominiums which dot the grounds.

Most of these buildings house year-round residents; however, about 50 condominiums remain available through a rental pool. The accommodations range from studios to three-bedroom units, with the loft condos representing great bargains for the traveling couple. The lofts feature completely stocked modern kitchens, two bathrooms, living room/dining room combinations and private decks.

In addition to a well-groomed 18-hole championship golf course, Sudden Valley boasts tennis courts, a play barn, a recreation room, swimming pools, a marina, 22 parks, two beaches and an extension of the Whatcom County Library System. As well as these amenities, the resort frequently schedules special events. In the past, hot air balloon rides, ski trips to Mt. Baker, arts and crafts classes, and hiking and camping trips have been offered.

The Clubhouse and the Conference Center pose alongside the golf course. Inside the Clubhouse are the registration desk and the resort's restaurant, which looks out over the course. Both the restaurant and the center are available to groups, which make up a large portion of Sudden Valley's guests.

Despite all of the activities here, Sudden Valley promises peaceful isolation from everyday madness. Its surroundings are pristine, creating a Northwest ambiance.

Travel Notes and Insider Tips

From I-5, exit onto Lakeway Drive. Travel east to the lake, then drive south on Lake Whatcom Boulevard to Sudden Valley's second gate and follow the signs to the Clubhouse.

The resort will be the center of activity; however, guests should investigate Bellingham. Old Town, which hosts several unique shops and eateries, is a good place to begin. For fishermen and those curious about the life cycle of salmon, the Bellingham Maritime Heritage Center at 1600 C Street makes an interesting side trip. A must visit for museum buffs is the Whatcom Museum of History and Art (676-6981). As well as being located in a historically significant building, the museum houses early Northwest photography, Northwest Indian and Eskimo artifacts, Northwest contemporary works of art, and historical exhibits. Western Washington University offers an array of Northwest architecture as well as sculptures by international artists which are certainly worth the trip. Sightseers and outdoors people must make the one-hour drive to Mt. Baker. Hiking and camping there rank with Washington's best, while skiing is excellent. The famous Ski to Sea Festival (734-1330) is held in early May.

Condominium rates range from $64 for a studio to $129 for a three-bedroom unit. The buildings alongside the resort's Lake Louise are the most scenically located. Lofts looking out on the golf course are also excellent. Dinner entrees range from $6.95 (pasta and light fare) to the market price for lobster. All prices are subject to change and are provided only for comparison.

Sudden Valley Resort
100 Sudden Valley
Bellingham, WA 98226
(206) 734-6430

Rosario Resort

Islands produce a magical quality – a sense of peace wrapped in mystery. In the traveler's mind's eye appear images of white sandy beaches, palm trees swaying in tropical breezes, deep-blue waters and bodies bronzed by the sun.

But huddled in the northern waters of Puget Sound, sandwiched between America's Strait of Juan de Fuca and Canada's Strait of Georgia, float the San Juan Islands. Here beaches are mostly rocky, cool Northwest winds whisper through the tops of evergreens, the waters are often gray and shrouded in mist, and pale bodies usually outnumber those with tans. Yet the magic abounds.

Each day, Washington State Ferries ply narrow channels, bridging the waters to four of the islands – Lopez, Shaw, Orcas and San Juan – from Anacortes and the mainland. These ferries transport everything from tourists to supplies.

Horseshoe-shaped Orcas is the chain's most popular destination point. Its mountainous terrain harbors deep bays etched between rocky headlands, white shale beaches and a fiord-like bay that nearly cuts the island in half.

Perched atop a bluff overlooking the entrance to this bay sits the white gabled mansion of Rosario Resort. Overhead, puffy white clouds laced with shades of gray float lazily across a blue backdrop, while in the waters below white sails balloon toward a hilly horizon and sleek yachts cruise cautiously into the marina.

The mansion, a Mediterranean-style villa, is the legacy of shipbuilding magnate Robert Moran. He came to the island from Seattle in 1904 in order to live out his life on an island hideaway. Like Moran's ships, the mansion was built to endure and to exhibit class.

Workers chiseled the foundation from bedrock, the first two stories were made of solid concrete, and the roof was fabricated with six tons of sheet copper. Inside, walls were made of polished mahogany and parquet floors handcrafted of teakwood. The Music Room was graced with a Tiffany chandelier, a stained-glass window picturing the harbor at Antwerp, and mahogany-paneled cabinets encasing 1,972 pipes of an Aeolian organ.

Today the mansion still reflects elegance, and the Music Room remains a focal point of the resort. In addition, the villa houses Rosario's reception desk, a restaurant, a lounge, an indoor pool, a sauna and a whirlpool.

However, due to fire and safety regulations, the mansion's guest rooms are history. The 180 accommodations now available sit in wooden motel-like structures which dot the manicured lawns and the wooded hillsides around the villa. Their decor leans toward modest and some of the older buildings show wear. Nevertheless, the rooms are spacious and comfortable.

The real treasures at Rosario, besides the environment, are the year-round resort activities. There are three pools, a sauna, a whirlpool, a game room, tennis

courts, a nearby golf course, boating, fishing and early-evening organ concerts in the Music Room. And since 1985, Rosario has offered a spa featuring aerobics, massages, facials, pedicures, manicures and suntanning sessions.

The setting here is magical, the amenities are limitless. It is everything an island traveler could ask for from an island which sits distant miles from the Caribbean.

Travel Notes and Insider Tips

Washington State Ferries (464-6400) depart regularly from Anacortes, which is about a 90-minute drive north from Seattle. Take I-5 to Highway 20 west. Seattle's Lake Union Air Service (284-2784) and San Juan Airlines (622-6077) also serve the resort.

Very little rain falls in the San Juans and temperatures are usually moderate. Yet water-resistant walking shoes and warm sweaters are advised for those who wish to explore the island. Nearby Moran State Park is the best place to begin an island tour. A tower atop 2,400-foot Mount Constitution offers sweeping views of the San Juans. For a real taste of the island, however, visit the tiny waterfront community of Olga. Fishermen will be delighted to know that the waters surrounding Orcas teem with sea bass, cod, snapper and salmon. People and scenery watchers should grab a sandwich at The Hungry Whale in Orcas Landing, where the ferries dock. Shoppers should investigate Eastsound's gift shops and the many arts and crafts galleries dotting Orcas.

Rosario's most private accommodations sit atop the hill overlooking the manicured grounds. Rooms 2110 and 2115 feature full kitchens, fireplaces, separate bedrooms and living rooms, and great views. Below the hill, buildings 2300 and 2400 house ten fireplace units and are the resort's newest facilities. Closer to the mansion but still offering good views are units 1305-07 and 1314-16. Double room rates vary greatly but generally begin at $83. The fare in the Orcas Room is continental and moderately priced. The steaks are usually excellent. All prices are subject to change and are provided only for comparison.

Rosario Resort
Eastsound, WA 98245
(206) 376-2222
(800) 562-8820 (Inside Washington)

Roche Harbor Resort

Peace, beauty and rejuvenation – the traveler's trilogy – bring vacationers by the thousands to the San Juan Islands. Island travelers often begin their search at the end of the ferry line – San Juan Island.

As the ferry slides into its Friday Harbor berth, passengers scramble to the floating parking lot below deck. While tourists invade, local life continues unabated: Herons and gulls squabble over breakfast, sailors amble through forests of masts bobbing in the marina, anglers putt across San Juan Channel, and townsfolk exchange news and gossip in the San Juan Island Donut Shop. There is a sense of ease, a feeling of friendliness wafting through the maritime air.

"You know, San Juan Islanders are mostly of fishing and farming stock," explains Bette Rice, co-owner of a local bed and breakfast. "These people just seem to be friendly by nature."

And nature is what this island really advertises. San Juan's 56 square miles present a panoply of landscapes for auto tourists and bicyclists. Country roads bordered by sun-warmed fields and pastures crisscross the island's heart. Kaleidoscopic expanses of lavendar lupine and poppies in orange, red and white color the scene. Horses, cows and sheep munch windswept grasses. Bees buzz in the stillness, and white farmhouses garnish valley floors.

Rocky beaches littered with driftwood line San Juan's south side from Cattle Point to False Bay. Gnarled and wind-battered firs stand over waves of grass which climb steadily from the beaches to the bluffs. Rabbits and ferrets scamper about the grasslands, European skylarks sing in the trees, and bald eagles soar high above. Freighters trailing smoke cruise through the dark strait. On the distant shore, snow-mantled mountains stand against the horizon.

Only a few minutes away – but poles apart from the small-town atmosphere of Friday Harbor, the pastoral simplicity of San Juan Valley and the beachcomber ambiance permeating San Juan's south side – rests Roche Harbor. Located at the island's northwest tip, the resort offers travelers a cosmopolitan lifestyle wrapped in bucolic surroundings. While diners dressed in sportswear sip wine and sunbathe on the restaurant's wooden deck, yachts slip in and out of the marina, bathers splash in the nearby pool and walkers stroll through the flourishing flower garden.

Roche Harbor's beginnings date back to 1886, when it was founded by John S. McMillan to serve as a company town for the Roche Harbor Lime and Cement Company. At the turn of the century he built the ivy-clad Hotel de Haro to host his wealthy and important friends, who included Teddy Roosevelt.

Today, weeds climb the cold kilns and trees hide the scarred slopes of this once-prosperous lime operation.

But the hotel still welcomes guests, and the grounds continue to echo with visitors. In fact, the hotel looks much the same as it did when President Roosevelt stayed here in 1906. Its 20 guest rooms creak with age, while offering glimpses into the past.

However, for all but sentimentalists and history buffs, the resort's Lagoon Shore Condominiums make for a much more comfortable stay. These natural wood structures pose under a canopy of evergreens, offer views of the harbor and feature splendid amenities. Fireplaces, private decks, modern kitchens and large bathrooms adorn the facilities. In many ways, these are the best resort accommodations in Washington.

In addition to the hotel and the condominiums, Roche Harbor has several cozy cottages perched at the northern end of the grounds. They look out over the swimming pool, tennis courts and recreation yard to the harbor. However, these private little hideaways boast such popularity that reservations are booked months, sometimes a year, in advance.

Roche Harbor has become a haven for boaters who appreciate the dock moorage for some 200 boats as well

as the availability of service and supplies. Yet this resort is a great place for anyone wanting to get away. It doesn't offer all the activities of some resorts, but Roche Harbor does promise scenic serenity.

Travel Notes and Insider Tips

San Juan Island can be reached by Washington State Ferry (464-6400), Seattle's Lake Union Air Service (284-2784) or San Juan Airlines (622-6077). The ferry dock is in Anacortes, 90 minutes north of Seattle.

Exploring is the favorite activity here outside of boating and fishing. History abounds at the National Historical Park. Here, though at opposite ends of the island, rest American and English Camps, legacies of the Pig War (a non-war beginning with the death of a pig). A good driving tour of the island begins in Friday Harbor. Take Cattle Point Road to Cattle Point (the southeast tip of the island), then backtrack to American Camp Road. Access Cattle Point Road again and follow it to False Bay Drive. Where False Bay Drive meets Bailer Hill Road, turn left and stay on this road until it dead-ends at Lime Kiln Lighthouse. Here, get out of the car and walk about. This is a good place for a picnic. Back in Friday Harbor, be sure to visit The Whale Museum. The San Juan Island Dixieland Jazz Festival (378-5509), a celebration of good times, is held in late July.

Room rates are seasonal and weekend packages are available. Generally, the hotel ranges from $30 to $80, the condominiums from $60 to $130, and the cottages, which require minimum four-night stays in July and August, run anywhere from $60 to $85 per night. Food on the island, including the resort, is moderately priced but average in quality at best. All prices are subject to change and are provided only for comparison.

Roche Harbor Resort
P.O. Box 1
Roche Harbor, WA 98250
(206) 378-2155

Mountain Home Lodge

Mountain Home isn't much as far as mountains go: Its rounded top stands just 2,500 feet. But at the 2,200-foot level stands a three-story cedar lodge which presents environs usually reserved only for hikers and climbers willing to sweat and scratch their way to isolated heights.

Here the air is fresh and clear, scented with cedar and pine. Only the moos of cows in the valley far below and the buzzing of bees flitting from wildflower to wildflower interrupt the stillness. Evergreens encircle the sloping meadow, while in the distance Stuart Range, pleated and imposing, juts its peaks into puffs of gray. Despite the cooling mountain breezes, the sun brings warmth over the entire scene.

Standing in the corner of this portrait – at the end of a winding and narrow two-and-one-half-mile washboard, referred to by locals as a road – sits Mountain Home Lodge. Along its upper deck rise blue and white umbrellas which shade patio tables and canvas chairs. To the right, stairs descend to a Jacuzzi and a swimming pool which center the lower deck.

At the second-floor level, a screen door enters the lodge's combination living room/dining room. Dark open beams support polished pine boards framing a canted ceiling. Sun splashes through a bank of cathedral windows. Opposite the windows, a tiered stone fireplace dominates a sitting area marked by three redwood burl sofas, each covered with a sheepskin. Looking out toward the range, eight oak tables await diners. Green plants flourish; classical music sets the tone.

Eight guest rooms sit on the second and third floors. A short hall leads from the second-floor foyer to two suites. Both are roomy and have private entrances. Only suite one, however, features views of the range.

Plush camel carpet covers stairs leading to the third-floor rooms. Canted pine ceilings, open beams, pine and walnut furniture, antique beds and lots of natural light highlight the rooms. All have private bathrooms, while rooms three and four offer mountain vistas.

While summer is a good time to visit – especially for hiking, fishing, climbing or sightseeing – Mountain Home Lodge becomes a special getaway once snow carpets the ground. Then guests leave their cars at the bottom of the mountain and are loaded aboard a snowcat for a ride to the lodge.

From December until late March or early April, winter fun abounds. Alongside the lodge stretches a 1,700-foot toboggan run, which rockets guests down a chute to a powdery stop just at the edge of snow-draped evergreens. Cross-country skiing, however, is the headliner here. Skiers have access to 50 kilometers of groomed trails which wind through tall forests and along steep ridges. The innkeepers will shuttle the advanced skiers, their equipment, plus lunch and hot drinks, to the top of Wedge Mountain for an eight-mile run back to the lodge.

Mountain Home Lodge's intimate size and lofty location make it unique among year-round getaways in this area. It is hard to imagine a better way to commune with Washington's Cascades.

Travel Notes and Insider Tips

The lodge is located just east of downtown Leavenworth off of Highway 2. From the west, drive through Leavenworth, across the Wenatchee River to a right on Duncan Road, which connects with Mountain Home Road. From the east, turn left on Duncan Road. In the winter, parking is at the entrance to Duncan Road.

In the winter, guests will likely remain at the lodge, using its facilities during their stay. But downhill skiers will want to venture to nearby Stevens Pass or Mission Ridge. When weather warms, guests should explore the area. Leavenworth is a Bavarian town geared to tourists. As well as lots of unique shops, the town hosts several festivals: the Christmas Lighting Festival in early December, Washington State Autumn Leaf Festival begining late September and Mai-Fest in mid-May. White-water rafting is excellent on the Wenatchee River between Leavenworth and Cashmere. Trout fishing is good at Fish Lake, the Alpine Lakes and Lake Wenatchee. World-class rock climbing is available at several sites along Icicle River Road out of Leavenworth and at the Dryden Pinnacles just west of Cashmere. In Cashmere, be sure to visit the Chelan County Historical Museum and the Aplets and Cotlets Candy Kitchen. This area features outstanding fall colors: Tumwater Canyon, west of Leavenworth, offers excellent displays of coloring. This is also orchard country. Fruit stands dot either side of Highway 2.

Food at the lodge is a daily set menu and is quite good. In summer, meals are optional and reservations for dinner must be made 24 hours in advance. Rates per person are $7.50 for breakfast, $5 for lunch and $17.50 for dinner. Doubles range from $58 to $78. In winter, rates include all meals and run from $118 to $138. Winter reservations should be made three to six months in advance. All prices are subject to change and are provided only for comparison.

Mountain Home Lodge
P.O. Box 687
Leavenworth, WA 98826
(509) 548-7077

Whaley Mansion

When travelers ponder Chelan, two thoughts predominate – sun and water. Central Washington's arid climate provides the glow, some 300 days of it, while fiord-like Lake Chelan supplies Adam's wine.

Chelan's charms regularly lure more than 125,000 summer visitors to this tiny town of 3,100 residents. Nestled at the foot of 55-mile-long Lake Chelan, the village rests in the midst of furrowed mountains and hillside orchards.

Along with sun-worshipers and sightseers, romantics have been coming to Chelan for years. Now for the first time, however, this scenic spot features a place designed especially with Cupid in mind – Whaley Mansion. A night at owner Mary Kay's bed-and-breakfast inn resembles a close encounter with an ornate valentine.

Upon entering the three-story white frame house, guests find themselves in a world of fantasy. Mary Kay has decorated her home to resemble a vision: It recalls the elegance and romance of her grandmother's time. The setting sparkles with cut-glass bowls, crystal goblets and Wedgwood china; it warms with French wallpaper, teal blue carpet and slab tiger oak trim. For some, the antiques and heirlooms may seem too museum-like, while for others, the environment may provide just the right ingredients for kindling tender feelings.

Six bedrooms make up the upper two floors. Iron beds, plush carpets, delicate wallpapers, warm colors, brass fixtures, ruffled fabrics, silk flowers, satiny sheets, polished woods, charming antiques and walls of shiny mirrors create an ambiance totally unique in the Northwest. The surroundings provide a haven for romance.

Travel Notes and Insider Tips

From Spokane take U.S. 2 west to Orondo then north on State Highway 151 to Chelan. From Seattle take I-90 to U.S. 97 north to Chelan. Third Street intersects U.S. 97. Look for the Whaley Mansion sign on the west side of the highway.

All outdoor activities are popular here, including hiking, skiing, swimming, boating, fishing, horseback riding, tennis and golf. Sightseers must board the Lady of the Lake II (682-2224) for an excursion to Stehekin, located at the opposite end of the lake. Round trips are scheduled but make up a long day. Check with Chelan Airways (682-5555) for return trips. See pages 70 and 71 for more tips on Chelan.

Doubles range from a winter low of $45 to a summer high of $95, breakfast included. All prices are subject to change and are provided only for comparison.

**Whaley Mansion
415 Third Street
Chelan, WA 98816
(509) 682-5735**

Campbell's Lodge

Campbell's Lodge is a sprawling lakeside resort that just grew and grew and grew.

The lodge began modestly enough. In 1889, C.C. Campbell, a 34-year-old lawyer from Iowa, arrived in the Chelan Valley seeking his fortune. He liked what he saw and began purchasing town lots.

Seeing the need for a hostelry, C.C. erected a hotel on a commanding site. Located by Lake Chelan, it both overlooked magnificent scenery and intercepted freight wagons just before they crossed the Chelan River. In addition to putting up teamsters and drivers, the hotel became an overnight stop for people traveling uplake by steamer. The Campbell Hotel, later known as The Campbell House, enjoyed immediate popularity and success.

Today that original three-story barn-like building still serves as the resort's focal point, though due to a fire and old age guests no longer stay there. Nevertheless, it still stands as Chelan's tallest building, and the flagpole sprouting from its angular roof continues to represent one of the town's oldest landmarks.

Growth and expansion began in the 1940s. Alongside The Campbell House, which now houses the restaurant and lounge, stretches a series of motels and frame cottages. From the parking lot side, they mirror any motel sprawling along any highway in America.

But stepping through the units to the lakeside is like walking into a sun-worshiper's dream. Giant poplars and shapely locusts shade manicured lawns, swimming pools and sandy beaches. Scantily clad bodies of every age, shape and size play and tan under blue skies. Sailboats, yachts, fishing craft and wind-surfers ply the shimmering waters.

Nearby, the brown hills of Washington's desert roll above the lake's southern shores. Giant boulders blemish their furrows, while orchards spot the slopes with green patches. In the opposite direction, the 55-mile-long lake sticks its arm into the Cascade Mountains, where towering peaks disappear into the clouds.

Accommodations here are difficult to describe because they are so varied. They range from a standard motel room to a two-bedroom beach cottage with a fireplace. The room decor runs from contemporary to '50s mix and match. All the units have electric heat, air conditioning and private baths. In addition, except for cottages 16 through 20, all have televisions, telephones and water views. (Room 200 has a television and a telephone but no view.)

As well as featuring pleasant surroundings, the resort's restaurant offers good food. The chefs describe the fare as wholesome and unpretentious. They pull it off by using simple and fresh ingredients.

Actually, the food preparation makes a statement about Campbell's philosophy: This resort is understated. Modest but comfortable accommodations, a family environment, caring service and magnificent scenery combine to make the resort one of Washington's finest.

Travel Notes and Insider Tips

From Seattle, take I-90 to Cle Elum. Here, pick up State 970 to U.S. 97 north. A more scenic route would be to take I-405 to State 522, which accesses U.S. 2. This then becomes Highway 97. From Spokane, take either I-90 to U.S. 97 or Highway 2 to State 151 north. From Portland, take I-84 to U.S. 97 north. In the summer, those driving from Vancouver can take State 20 to Twisp, then State 153 to Highway 97 south. Chelan Municipal Airport is paved and lit.

Sightseers should visit Ohme Gardens just outside Wenatchee. The environment is like that of an alpine meadow. Nearby Rocky Beach Dam features exhibits of Columbia River history and eye-to-eye views of salmon and steelhead. Lake Chelan is one of the most popular summer getaways in Washington. Besides swimming, fishing, boating and water skiing, there are magnificient views. One of the best is atop a hill on No-See-Um Road. Some of the area's best trout fishing is on Wapato Lake. Stop at Kelly's Hardware in Chelan and ask local legend Lee Fairchild for tips. The Lake Chelan Municipal Golf Course is five minutes from the resort. For boaters, Campbell's has moorage for 24 boats.

As well as hosting leisure travelers, Campbell's offers excellent facilities and catering services to groups. For those guests who enjoy setting up housekeeping, the cottages are superb. These need to be reserved a year in advance. July and August are the resort's busiest months. May, June, September and October can be excellent times to visit. There is a wide range of rates here. For example, a standard queen is $28 in the off-season but $86 in July and August. Cottages range from $54 to $140 per night, with six-night minimum stays in July and August. Dinner entrees go from $8.50 to $12.50. All prices are subject to change and are provided only for comparison.

Campbell's Lodge
P.O. Box 278
Chelan, WA 98816
(509) 682-2561

LAKE CHELAN WASHINGTON

Inn of the White Salmon

The smells pouring from the kitchen cast spells on visitors to this bed-and-breakfast inn. Aromas of baking bread, apples, peaches and cinnamon flavor the air. It's like sitting in grandma's old-fashioned kitchen, sipping tea and playing a round of cribbage, while her sweets puff and brown in the oven nearby.

No other inn can boast of such a remarkable kitchen. While most bed and breakfasts thrive on down comforters and priceless antiques, breakfasts have rocketed the Inn of the White Salmon into the guest house hall of fame. Its bounty and quality draw rave reviews from newspapers and magazines throughout the area. Surprisingly, this gustatory extravaganza began as only a snack.

When the inn first opened in 1978, Bill Hopper, co-owner and husband of chef extraordinaire Loretta, suggested a continental breakfast. "I think coffee and rolls would be nice," was how he put it. So in the early days, guests received this continental offering on a Sears card table set up in the lobby – paper plates and plastic forks accompanied the fare.

But Loretta, who honed her cooking skills in an Akron, Ohio, Polish neighborhood, quickly tired of this arrangement. Then the breakfast scene moved from the lobby to a new dining room, linen tablecloths and heirloom china displaced paper and plastic, and the kitchen began cooking home-baked delicacies.

Today an expansive buffet greets breakfast guests with some 40 pastries, from cream cheese and raisin strudel, to Alsatian apple tarts. But that's not all. In addition, breakfast includes six to eight egg dishes, several kinds of juice and a variety of fresh fruit.

Although all the guest accommodations don't yet equal the quality of the breakfasts, continual upgrading of the inn's 20 rooms reflects progress toward that goal. The Hoppers have worked hard to civilize a rather ordinary brick building, which served as a nondescript hotel for 40 years.

Today hostesses clad in long skirts and puff-sleeved blouses welcome guests to the inn. The lobby exudes a turn-of-the-century look. Time-honored photographs, a beveled mirror, antique chairs and a 1905 cash register adorn the area. Most guest rooms boast portraits and paintings of flowers and landscapes, floral-print wallpaper, antique dressers and queen-size beds. Amenities include color televisions, room telephones, large soft towels and a Jacuzzi on the back deck. Every room, except 203, features a private bathroom.

While nearly every bed and breakfast proves to be a unique experience, few offer the Inn of the White Salmon's special blend of mountain scenery, charming decor and gourmet food.

Travel Notes and Insider Tips

From Portland, follow I-84 to Hood River, then take Exit 64 north across the Columbia River to Bingen. Next, take State 141 to White Salmon. The inn is the last large building on the right. From Seattle, take I-5 to I-205, then State 14 to State 141.

The inn is ideally located for both the Columbia Gorge and the Cascade Mountains. Sightseers should hike to the top of 848-foot Beacon Rock and also visit Bonneville Dam. Both are located alongside State 14, west of Bingen. This entire area is rich in recreational opportunities: cross-country skiing at Trout Lake, downhill skiing at Mount Hood, rafting on the White Salmon and Klickitat rivers, and guided fishing trips with Columbia Scenic Gorge Excursions. Shoppers will find many unique outlets in both Bingen and White Salmon. For more tips see pages 28, 29 and 73.

The inn's double rates, which include breakfast, range from a low of $60 (Room 203) to a high of $130 (honeymoon suite with a fireplace and a hot tub); winter rates are slightly lower. Children are not permitted on weekends. All prices are subject to change and are provided only for comparison.

Inn of the White Salmon
172 Jewett Street
White Salmon, WA 98672
(509) 493-2335

Three Creeks Lodge

No one has ever confused Goldendale with either Paris or New York. The idea of a romantic evening set in posh surroundings seems as remote to that little farming community as does a hay ride down the Champs Élysées or a tractor pull down Madison Avenue. Yet romance is where you find it, and these days Cupid can be found slinging his arrows at a little resort just eight miles north of Goldendale.

Set within the pine and fir forests of southern Washington's Simcoe Mountains, Three Creeks Lodge seems as good a place as any to kindle a fire but an unlikely site to find elegance. However, owners Colin and Judith Chisholm have created a getaway package which yields an environment filled with class. They have blended a lot of country with a restaurant boasting gourmet food, called it "A Memorable Evening," and pulled off a coup in the resort industry.

It begins with checking into a modern chalet, built of cedar and tucked into the woods alongside the Little Klickitat River. Washing through a skylight in the canted ceiling, the sun splashes across a decor dominated by ponderosa pine. A large sliding glass door leads outside onto a private deck shaded by thick woods. The afternoon demands a leisurely pace, perhaps a dip in the spa or a walk along the river.

When evening arrives, jeans are cast aside for more formal attire – a suit for him, a dress for her. The restaurant, which sits only a few feet from the chalet, awaits the couple. Inside the cedar and pine board building, classical music and quiet conversation promote a serene mood.

When the couple arrives, the maître d', looking dapper in his blue suit, escorts them to their table. A linen tablecloth and a glass candelabrum garnish the setting. With dash and flair he spreads napkins on their laps and hands the lady a single red rose. For the next two hours the maître d' serves them a seven-course dinner from a tableside flambé cart.

As enchanting as this may sound, it's not necessary to partake of this special package to enjoy either the bucolic lodging or the gourmet food. Since opening in 1984, Three Creeks Lodge has gained quick popularity among both guests and diners. While the 12 chalet units are comfortable and offer amenities such as electric heat, telephones, televisions and in some cases spas and kitchenettes, it is the food here that ranks as special.

Besides fresh local ingredients, stone-ground wheat for rolls and breads, fresh-ground coffee and homemade ice cream, the menu features a wide range of choices. Especially good are the fruits de mer (scallops, shrimp, salmon and crab prepared in a béchamel sauce and served in a shell) and the poached fillet of salmon served in a lime and walnut butter sauce. For some, the flambés may be overpowered by brandy, but in general the food is excellent here.

Three Creeks is ideally located for year-round seasonal activities. In the summer the Columbia Gorge features sightseeing, fishing, boating and rafting, while in the winter the mountains host cross-country skiing and snowmobiling. As well as boasting advantages, however, the location also makes up the lodge's only drawback: It sits along busy Highway 97. A bluff shelters guests from the sights of 18-wheelers but not from their sounds. Nevertheless, the intrusion is slight.

In the past, southern Washington has had some difficulty attracting tourists. Three Creeks Lodge may be just one more reason why that trend has been changing in recent years.

Travel Notes and Insider Tips

From Seattle or Spokane, travelers can take I-90 to I-82, then Highway 97 south to five miles beyond Satus Pass. From Portland, take I-84 to Highway 97 north. Goldendale has an airport with a 3,600-foot lighted runway.

This area teems with things to do. Sightseers and art lovers must visit both Maryhill Museum of Art and the Stonehenge Monument located alongside Highway 14. Just on the edge of town sits the Goldendale Observatory (773-3141), home of the nation's largest telescope which is available to the public. Within an hour's drive of the lodge sprawls the Yakima Valley wine country. Some 12 wineries welcome visitors. Fishermen will discover good salmon and steelhead fishing in the Klickitat River, excellent trout fishing in the Klickitat and White Salmon Rivers, and sturgeon fishing in the Columbia River. Trout Lake also has good fishing in addition to being a bird sanctuary. For golfers, there is a 9-hole course in Goldendale.

Lodging rates here run from $42 to $104 for doubles. Special packages are available. Dinner entrees range from $9.95 to $18.50. A Memorable Evening is $32.50 per person, excluding lodging. All prices are subject to change and are provided only for comparison.

Three Creeks Lodge
2120 Highway 97
Goldendale, WA 98620
(509) 773-4026

Spokane

This city of 172,000 suffers from an image problem. Few travelers think of Spokane as either a town of beauty or one of interest. Even a World's Fair, a 1975 selection as an All America city and a citing by the National Association of Realtors in 1977 for its downtown revitalization have failed to spark enthusiasm. All of this is unfortunate, because Spokane is a city worth discovery.

Located on the edge of Washington's wheat country and just 18 miles west of Idaho, Spokane ranks as the largest city between Minneapolis and Seattle. Because of its location and its size, the "Lilac City" has become the service and trade center for an 80,000-square-mile area which stretches from the Cascades to the Rockies. This translates into a vibrant city, capable of hosting and entertaining both business and leisure travelers.

The compact downtown is bordered on the south by Interstate 90 and on the north by the Spokane River. Automobile access along one-way streets makes driving simple, but the downtown area should be explored on foot.

Begin at Riverfront Park, site of the 1974 World's Fair. Its 53-acre grounds are marked by the boiling rapids of Spokane Falls, islands of rolling lawns and a 1909 hand-carved carousel.

For shopping along Spokane's skywalk, the nation's second-largest such system, start at nearby city hall and cross over to River Park Square. From there, the skywalk bridges numerous stores and restaurants, including JC Penney and The Bon Marche.

An automobile comes in handy for seeing the rest of Spokane. Manito Park, which welcomes more than 100,000 visitors annually, is Spokane's showcase oasis.

It sprawls between 17th and 25th Avenues along Grand Boulevard. The park features 18th-century-style Duncan Gardens, a Japanese garden and a conservatory. Fans of Bing Crosby will want to drive out Boone Avenue to Gonzaga University, site of the Crosby Library. Bing grew up at East 508 Sharp and was a student at Gonzaga. Nearby is the Museum of Native American Cultures. This five-story building sits on the banks of the Spokane River and features an outstanding collection of Indian artifacts and Western art.

All in all, Spokane offers a great deal to see and do. It may not have the sophistication or natural beauty of Vancouver, Seattle, or even Portland, but Spokane has a pulse of its own that is unique to the region.

Travel Notes and Insider Tips

Interstate 90 cuts through Spokane. Travelers heading west should exit Division, Lincoln or Cedar; those driving east should exit Walnut or Division.

Gourmet dining isn't abundant in Spokane, but good food amidst pleasant surroundings is available at Moreland's (747-9830) and Patsy Clark's (838-8300). Recreational opportunities include golf at Indian Canyon Municipal Golf Course, downhill and cross-country skiing at Mt. Spokane State Park and horse racing at Playfair. The Spokane Civic Theater (325-2507) presents live theater year-round. The Flour Mill, which ground its last flour in 1973, overlooks Riverfront Park and today houses 26 shops and restaurants, including the Book and Game Company. The Spokane Lilac Festival (624-1393) is held in mid-May.

For more information, contact the Spokane Regional Convention and Visitors Bureau, West 301 Main, Spokane, WA 99201 (624-1341). All of the above numbers are in area code 509.

Cavanaugh's Inn at the Park

Inn at the Park may be the new kid on the block, but it is wasting no time becoming the leader of the pack. The hotel's aggressive management recognizes Spokane's increasingly growing role as a convention and trade center. Spurred by this corporate activity, growth and expansion dominate the hotel's plans.

The original 186-room inn opened April 6, 1983. Although not centrally located in downtown, its riverfront perch offers guests an environment previously unavailable in Spokane. In addition, a footbridge connects the four-story ziggurat-shaped building with Riverfront Park, which sprawls just minutes from the city's financial district.

The hotel reaches out to all people. For corporate travelers and local business people it features 11 meeting and banquet rooms designed to accommodate groups from ten to 1,100. As well as corporate rates, the inn offers frequent business guests a free gold card. This card provides travelers additional benefits such as express check-in and 30 percent discounts on meeting rooms. Finally, service, which is so essential to corporate travelers, is fast, friendly and efficient.

Despite the fact that most of the hotel's business is corporate (true of most hotels), the inn's location and infrastructure also cater to the leisure traveler. Looking out across the Spokane River as it froths green through the park, while joggers, walkers and marmots crisscross amongst the trees, the hotel boasts an environment typical of resorts rather than hotels. Its low rates for standard rooms also act as incentives to vacationers.

Amenities here pose attractively to both kinds of travelers. The lobby, Garden Lounge and Atrium Cafe & Deli bathe in the natural light cascading through a solarium. Tropical vegetation and rattan chairs adorn the cafe, while off to one side rich leather chairs cozy up to a stone fireplace. In the afternoon the smells of steaming tea and hot buttered scones announce afternoon tea.

More elegant dining takes place in the Windows of the Seasons Restaurant, which overlooks the river and the park. Wicker chairs, linen tablecloths, pile carpeting and fresh flowers garnish the terraces. This upscale look continues in the Park Place Lounge, which neighbors the restaurant and features nightly music.

The inn's rooms, while comfortable, cannot be considered elegant. Their modest decor mirrors the better rooms found in motels. However, in 1986 the new 85-room Executive Tower opened, offering both more luxury and better amenities.

"We're trying to create the best of all worlds," General Manager Arthur Coffey says. "The corporate traveler needs a more elegant, quieter place, like the Executive Tower. Many of our other guests appreciate the lower rates and facilities for parties that are found in the main hotel."

Besides enjoying the ambiance of the park, the hotel offers several leisure activities. In the inn there are two outdoor pools, several whirlpools and an exercise room. The first floor of the tower hosts a fitness facility. It boasts an indoor lap pool, a dry sauna, a suntanning room, a weight room and a Jacuzzi.

Trying to be everything to everybody sometimes translates into lots of nothing. However, there is a sense that the Inn at the Park will succeed. So far the hotel is heading in the right direction.

Travel Notes and Insider Tips

From I-90, take Exit 281 to Division Street. After crossing the river, turn left onto North River Drive to the hotel.

Most of the inn's rooms are quiet; however, you may wish to avoid the accommodations which are directly above the lounge. Food in the Seasons Restaurant is very good and generally equals anything to be found downtown in both price and quality. Service here is first-class: The entire staff seems eager to meet the needs of their guests. Although the inn isn't your typical luxury hotel, visitors here tend to be upscale and their attire reflects that. Nevertheless, leisure dress is acceptable. See page 74 for things to do and places to see in Spokane.

Room rates for doubles at the inn range from $64.50 to $250. There are two Jacuzzi Suites that rent for $185. Many of the rooms here look out over a large parking lot, so ask for a room on the river's side. Doubles in the tower run around $85 to $100. Dinner entrees in the Seasons Restaurant average $12.95. All prices are subject to change and are provided only for comparison.

Cavanaugh's Inn at the Park
West 303 North River Drive
Spokane, WA 99201-2286
(509) 326-8000

British Columbia

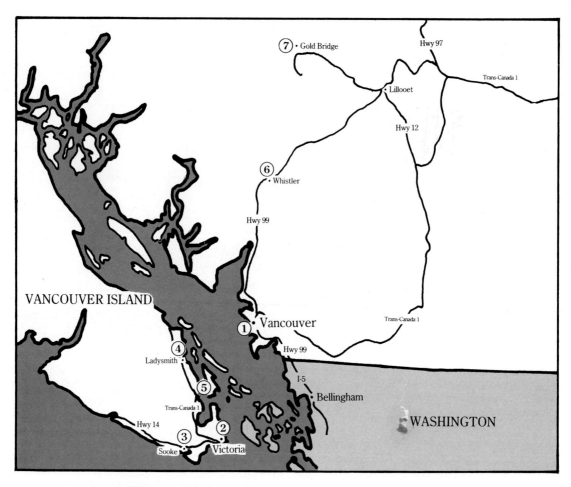

1. Four Seasons Hotel
   The Granville Island Hotel
   The Mandarin Vancouver
   Park Royal Hotel
   Wedgewood Hotel
2. The Beaconsfield Inn
   Oak Bay Beach Hotel

3. Sooke Harbour House
4. Yellow Point Lodge
5. Hastings House
6. Whistler
7. Little Gun Lake Lodge

For more information about British Columbia, write or call:

Tourism British Columbia
Robson Square
800 Hornby Street, Room 140
Vancouver, B.C., Canada V6Z 2C5
(604) 668-2861

Little Gun Lake, Gold Bridge, British Columbia

Shannon Falls, British Columbia

Chinatown, Vancouver, British Columbia

Yellow Point Lodge

Yellow Point Lodge brings real meaning to the words rustic and natural. Everything here pays tribute to the environment and nothing is ever done to disturb the fragile ecology of the place.

Entrance to this getaway tells travelers much about the kind of resort it is. Situated 15 miles southeast of Nanaimo, the lodge hides several twists and turns from Trans-Canada 1, the main highway along southeastern Vancouver Island. A narrow and furrowed dirt road cuts through dense fir and pine before reaching the doorstep of the lodge. It is at this time that visitors must pause, take check of their inner senses and commit to a backwoods experience.

The resort sits on a sandstone promontory of massive proportions. The blue-gray waters of Stuart Channel lap the outcropping, while red cedars shade the grounds. In the near distance the Gulf Islands' rolling hills enhance the feeling of isolation. Harlequin ducks and sea otters ply the channel; several bald eagles take to the wing. Somewhere on a distant horizon, the 20th century grinds away. But here, nature stands unassailable.

Until recently, a pine-timbered lodge, built in 1938 by Gerry Hill, stood on the promontory. In that lodge the atmosphere bordered on hypnotic: It was not unusual to see guests clad in sweat shirts and wool socks sipping tea, reading paperbacks, gazing seaward and napping peacefully. Unfortunately, fire destroyed this legendary landmark in October 1985. Today, the Friends of Yellow Point are working diligently to raise a new lodge from the ashes of the old one. By the spring of 1987, a rustic hideaway will once again peer out across the channel.

In the meantime, Yellow Point continues to offer guests rest and relaxation. A number of cabins, which escaped the fire, remain strewn about the resort's 180 acres. Some border on being primitive, and that seems to be the way most guests prefer it.

In fact, that's the key to Yellow Point's success: Keep it simple and allow people to discover themselves. That philosophy, with or without a main lodge, prospers here, drawing travelers of all kinds, from blue collar to wealthy executives. To most, Yellow Point offers the mind and nervous system the coddling of a special kind of health spa.

Ron, a photographer with the movie industry in Los Angeles, is typical of Yellow Point's guests: He came for a night and stayed for a week. "I can't leave," he explains. "I've discovered paradise and can't let go."

Travel Notes and Insider Tips

From Vancouver, take the Nanaimo ferry out of Horseshoe Bay. Once in Nanaimo, go south on Trans-Canada 1 for three miles to Cedar Road. Follow it to Yellow Point Road. From Portland, take the Black Ball ferry out of Port Angeles, Washington, to Victoria. Drive north to Ladysmith via Trans-Canada 1. Three miles beyond Ladysmith follow the signs to Yellow Point. NOTE: Once off the highway, back roads take over. It's best to get specific directions from the lodge.

Most guests will spend their time at Yellow Point. Facilities include a saltwater pool, two tennis courts, volleyball and badminton courts, a hot tub and a sauna. Activities feature beachcombing, hiking, sunbathing, boating, wind surfing, dancing, barbecuing and partying. However, guests should leave the premises at least once to visit Crow and Gate, British Columbia's first neighborhood pub.

The Beach Barracks, Beach Cabins and Field Cabins are primitive, with no running water. Rates run from $70 to $100. Two cottages cost $135 each. The other cabins, which share bathrooms, cost $105. All prices include meals. Guests must be over 16 and no pets are allowed. Minimum stays are required on weekends and holidays. This place enjoys year-round popularity, so book reservations well in advance. All prices are Canadian, subject to change and provided only for comparison.

Yellow Point Lodge
Rural Route 3
Ladysmith, B.C., Canada V0R 2E0
(604) 245-7422

Victoria

This Vancouver Island city's reputation as a peaceful and dignified haven germinated in 1843 on a quadrangular plot of grassland measuring 330 feet by 300 feet. In 1858, author Alfred Waddington described this developing colony, originally labeled Fort Victoria, as a place where there is "No noise, no bustle, no gamblers . . . a few gentlemanly behaved inhabitants . . . secluded as it were from the whole world." Victoria still stands rock-hard on that tranquil foundation.

In the 19th century, Victoria's peaceful pace, mild climate, protected harbor, unspoiled coastline and rolling hills lured moneyed European sophisticates – especially Londoners weary of fog and their drab, tired city. Before its 60th birthday, Victoria became both British and cultivated, boasting telephones, electric street lights, an electric transit system and a leisurely lifestyle symbolized by bowling on the green, cricket and afternoon tea.

Today the sophistication and pace still flourish, drawing nearly 2.2 million visitors annually. Tourists from around the world flock to this place of both man-made and natural beauty, escaping the frenzied pace of today's civilization.

Dozens of schooners and sloops, their sails full, pepper the waters of Victoria's inner harbor like whitecaps tossed up by a fresh breeze. Alongshore, the crowded marina tucks its curved shoulder into a city of modern high-rises and turn-of-the-century monoliths. The view is unobstructed – no smog, no pollutants stream skyward.

The ivy-covered walls of The Empress Hotel rise above the harbor. The building's peaked gables, copper cupolas – oxidized and splashed in turquoise – and steeply pitched slate roofs portend top-hat status. Cater-cornered from The Empress, the 23-karat-gilded statue of Capt. George Vancouver, surrounded by 33 weathered domes, stands atop the neo-Gothic Parliament Buildings.

Hanging flower baskets drape Victoria's street lamps, drawing attention to a symbol of early prosperity. Horses drawing Tally-Ho carriages clip-clop slowly up and down city streets, mindless of automobiles competing for space. Middle-aged men and women spend their days bowling on the green; more youthful souls indulge in cricket. Even tourists get caught up in the act – shunning motorized transportation for foot power or carriage and pausing to participate in the afternoon ritual of high tea.

Victoria caters to tourists and their needs. Locals smile and say hello; waiters and merchants offer honest assistance; city workers keep the streets and sidewalks clean; the visitors' bureau isn't hidden away on some seldom-traveled side street; and hotels and inns dress themselves in Sunday's best.

Travel Notes and Insider Tips

Several major airlines serve Seattle and Vancouver, where connections with smaller airlines may be made for the final jump to Victoria. Cars may be rented in both Seattle and Vancouver, then ferried across to the island. Ferries regularly leave from Port Angeles (206-457-4491), Seattle (206-623-5560), Anacortes (206-464-6400) and Tsawwassen, B.C. (604-669-1211).

Afternoon tea is a ritual that must be experienced. One of Victoria's best tearooms is The Bantley House Tearoom, several blocks from downtown on Fort Street. Be sure to visit the following sites: Butchart Gardens; Beacon Hill Park; the Crystal Garden, a tropical oasis complete with the flashing colors of macaws, pink Caribbean flamingos, speckled ringed teal ducks, goldfish and Japanese carp; the British Columbia Provincial Museum, considered among the world's best; the shops and restaurants along Government Street; Chinatown; and Fort Street, also known as Antique Row.

For more information about Victoria, write or call: Greater Victoria Visitor Information Centre, 812 Wharf Street, Victoria, B.C., Canada V8W 1T3 (604-382-2127).

Oak Bay Beach Hotel

These days first-class hotels seem to come in two flavors: shiny glass-and-steel high-rises which smack of new money and renovated duchesses which taste of old wealth. It's refreshing to find a venerable hotel which through the years has managed to maintain high standards without succumbing to modernization. That's the legacy of Victoria's Oak Bay Beach Hotel.

Since its opening in the 1930s, the hotel has cultivated an atmosphere of elegance. Afternoon tea and dining have always been taken seriously, and guests have come to expect character in their surroundings.

Today the same qualities permeate the environment, but the stuffiness is gone. Guests relax and talk animatedly while savoring high tea around the lobby's brick fireplace or on the patio overlooking the marina. White linen, crystal and china still grace the Tudor Room, but diners care more about the character of their wine than the cut of their neighbor's clothes.

This Tudor-style hotel has much to recommend it: The ambiance is old world, its 50 rooms meld antiques with modern conveniences, service is congenial and efficient, and its lounge is one of Victoria's most popular pubs. But none of these attributes challenge Oak Bay's location for top honors.

The hustle and bustle of tourism pulses at the opposite end of town. The Oak Bay Beach Hotel's black timbers and gables stand on the edge of a residential neighborhood; its back rises against the sea. Sailing yachts, fishing boats and dark freighters ply the waters between Discovery Island and the driftwood-littered beach. In the distance, Mt. Baker turns pink as the evening sun dips below Vancouver Island.

In addition to being Victoria's only seaside hotel, Oak Bay Beach boasts an amenity rare among its peers – a 41-foot yacht. The Mesouda, which is Egyptian for contented lady, stands ready for sightseeing cruises, fishing charters, business meetings and dinner parties.

The Oak Bay Beach Hotel's charms make it one of Victoria's most popular getaways. From mid-May to mid-October, rooms are often booked up to a year in advance. It is no wonder. Early on the hotel embraced high standards. Today's guests continue to receive the same care which made this hotel special 50 years ago.

Travel Notes and Insider Tips

From Victoria's inner harbor, take Belleville Street to Government. Turn left on Government, then drive right on Fort to Oak Bay Avenue. From Provincial 17, turn left on Johnson Street and follow it to Oak Bay Avenue.

Normally, visitors to Victoria are better off without their automobiles, but Oak Bay is a 15-minute drive from downtown, so cars provide a convenience recommended here. Limousine service is available, however, for a small charge. Oak Bay Village, a quaint community with interesting shops, is a ten-minute walk from the hotel. The nearby Oak Bay Recreation Centre offers spas, swimming, ice skating, tennis and curling. In addition, five public golf courses sprawl nearby.

Only some of the rooms here offer water views: None of the standards do. All accommodations include telephones, cable televisions and complimentary morning newspaper delivery. The best rooms are those suites with noble names such as The Victorian Suite, The Restoration Room and the King Henry VIII Room (no view, but the canopy bed is in a class by itself). Rates begin at $50 and go up to $225. Dinner entrees range from $12.45 to $22.85. All prices are Canadian, subject to change and provided only for comparison.

Oak Bay Beach Hotel
1175 Beach Drive
Victoria, B.C., Canada V8S 2N2
(604) 598-4556

The Beaconsfield Inn

Travelers from around the world come to Victoria to drink from its fountain of calm and to bathe in its more-English-than-England atmosphere. The Beaconsfield Inn, a recently renovated English heritage mansion, beckons guests to indulge in both activities.

Located only two blocks from downtown, the inn thrives on Victoria's image. Since its first guests arrived in 1984, The Beaconsfield has been recognized as Victoria's most elegant small hotel.

Humboldt Street is a quiet, tree-lined boulevard made up primarily of modern brick-and-concrete multi-story apartment complexes standing side by side on neat rectangular plots. Resting on a corner behind a black wrought-iron fence, The Beaconsfield, trimmed in burgundy, green and cream, forms the sort of juxtaposition common to Victoria's neighborhoods. It's not an unusual sight here to see stately older mansions rubbing shoulders with contemporary-style homes and apartments.

Originally built by millionaire R.P. Rithet as a wedding gift for his only daughter, Gertrude, the house once hosted Victoria's socialites and gentry. After Gertrude and her husband died, the mansion and its grounds deteriorated. Spiders replaced wealthy guests, and apartments sprouted instead of raspberries.

In 1982, Bill McKechnie, a soft-spoken man and current co-owner, saw the potential for an inn. "I love the challenge of bringing out the latent character of houses," he explains. So McKechnie, along with partner Stewart Lloyd, undertook restoration, using the original plans of architect Samuel McClure.

A few years later, the house displays its original Edwardian luster. A short garden path leads to the main entrance, which is dominated by a vaulted arch bearing the inn's name. Glass double doors, graced by a peacock's flowing plumage, open into the sun room. Rays of light cascade through the stained-glass windows and dance about the black-and-white checkerboard tile floor. Wicker chairs sit amongst potted plants.

A keen sense of masculine and feminine tastes historically marks Edwardian decor. Visitors to the main floor library can almost smell the cigars and taste the brandy. Its black leather couches, pressed back oak chairs, hardwood floor and red tile fireplace mirror an old English gentlemen's club.

On the other hand, the guest rooms reflect soft and subtle emotions. Lilly's room exemplifies the Edwardian sense of grace which permeates each of the inn's 12 guest rooms. Cream walls with white trim surround a mahogany queen-size tester bed resting on densely piled carpet. A simple, square brass light fixture hangs from the plaster ceiling. The bathroom (each accommodation has a private bath) features an old English tub, pedestal sink and steam-heated towel rack.

A small staff reflects the casual dress and informal behavior encouraged at The Beaconsfield. Smiles, handshakes and pots of tea welcome each guest. Although Westminster chimes ring in the hours, time matters little here.

Travel Notes and Insider Tips

From Victoria's inner harbor, take Belleville Street to a right on Douglas. Then turn left on Southgate, left on Quadra and right on Humboldt. From Provincial 17, follow Blanshard to a left on Humboldt.

The Beaconsfield stands within a 30-minute walk of most of Victoria's best sites. Don't miss the Emily Carr Gallery (an excellent small gallery) on Wharf Street, Harpo's for live music and dancing, and a fine English pub called Spinnakers. See page 79 for more tips.

All the rooms at The Beaconsfield are excellent. (Some include fireplaces.) Doubles, which include a full breakfast, range from $58 to $115. All prices are Canadian, subject to change and provided only for comparison.

The Beaconsfield Inn
998 Humboldt Street
Victoria, B.C., Canada V8V 2Z8
(604) 384-4044

Sooke Harbour House

Perched atop a grassy knoll on Vancouver Island's southern tip poses the quintessential portrait of a cozy country getaway – Sooke Harbour House. Located 23 miles west of Victoria, this small farmhouse sits undisturbed by modern intrusions.

The inn's surroundings paint a picture of peace. Below the house, green waves roll onto the rocky shore, while the noses of harbor seals look like black rubber balls bobbing in the water. To the left, Whiffen Spit carries its cargo of driftwood and shells across the harbor. In the distance, the Olympics' snowy peaks glisten above the Strait of Juan de Fuca.

Since 1980, owners Sinclair and Fredrica Philip have melded this environment with homey lodgings and culinary excellence. The results have produced a setting like that of a French auberge, where the rooms are comfortable and the food is superb.

The accommodations, five upstairs guest rooms, can be dispensed with quickly. They are modest, clean and comfortable but not special in the way of most great inns. Only the Blue Heron, a split-level suite which alone boasts a private bathroom, features any flair: An upper deck that looks out to sea, skylights sculptured in the cathedral ceiling and country pine furniture do invite pleasures other than sleeping.

However, the real joys here lie downstairs. You can smell them wafting from the kitchen, seeping out the windows and climbing the stairs. Their tentacles reach out and wrap the senses in gustatory heaven. Visitors may forget the guest rooms, may even have difficulty recalling the scenery, but the food at Sooke Harbour House is forever memorable.

Without overstating its quality, the fare reaches magnificent heights. Both the ingredients and preparation are unsurpassed. Food columnist John Doerper calls dining here "a rare culinary delight."

Served in two dining rooms which mirror country spaces, complete with fresh flowers and walls of windows, the Philips serve a cuisine described simply as Pacific Northwest. The menu continually changes to reflect the best available local ingredients.

Each day, local fishermen harvest their catch from nearby waters and rush it to the kitchen for dinner that evening. Sea urchin, sea cucumber and gooseneck barnacle fall prey to the scuba diving talents of Sinclair and his brother-in-law, Fred. Local farmers raise the restaurant's rabbit, lamb and suckling kid. Nearly all the vegetables and herbs sprout in the Philips' expansive gardens. Together these fresh foods, perfectly prepared, create a dining experience which sometimes lasts several hours.

Following dinner and before returning to Victoria or retiring upstairs, stuffed diners amble over to stuffed chairs. They sit around a granite fireplace, sip after-dinner drinks, share conversation and admire their contented bellies. Satisfaction appears in their smiles. Sooke Harbour claims a few more trophies in its memory case.

Travel Notes and Insider Tips

From Victoria, take Trans-Canada 1 to Highway 14. Drive west to Sooke, pass through the village and turn left at Whiffen Spit Road.

Dining is the major event here. Begin with either Sooke oysters in apple cider butter or local pink swimming scallops in a sabayan sauce. While each entree is superb, the salmon with fresh sorrel sauce and the suckling kid roasted with fresh herbs consistently earn rave reviews. All desserts are prepared fresh on the premises: The chocolate and walnut torte is particularly good. The wine list features a fine selection of British Columbian cottage wines and a select number of prestige wines. Besides eating, beachcombing and nature walks avail themselves. In July, barbecued salmon, Leechtown beef and bulky loggers highlight a local event called All Sooke Day. Call 642-6112 for information about this annual celebration or for more details about Sooke. See page 79 for tips on Victoria.

Room rates range from $30 to $87. Off-season rates are available. Dinner entrees range from $10 to $20. All prices are Canadian, subject to change and provided only for comparison.

Sooke Harbour House
1528 Whiffen Spit Road
Rural Route 4
Sooke, B.C., Canada V0S 1N0
(604) 642-3421

Vancouver

Throughout the years, Canadians and Americans have looked upon Vancouver as Canada's Pacific playground. Boasting a mild climate, 5,000-foot mountains, oceans of water, miles of beaches, acres of parks, a world of restaurants and a host of museums and art galleries, this perception seems natural. But Vancouver is much more than a Disney creation.

It's a city with a British heritage. Like Victoria, this lineage cultivated a sophistication and refinement often missing in the cities of North America. Perhaps more important, however, Vancouver is a city made up of the world's people. Its Chinatown is the second largest on the continent; Commercial Drive is home to some 50,000 residents of Italian extraction; and more than a third of Vancouver's children grow up in homes where English is a second language.

Beyond creating some problems of accommodation for the local government, this ethnic mix produces a city of energy – one that goes beyond a spirit of cosmopolitanism to the real thing. Foreign accents are as common as European labels; architecture is a careful blend of the old and the new; and the products of the world grace the shelves of downtown shops.

Before discovering Vancouver and exploring its heart, Stanley Park, visitors should survey its outer parts. The two best viewpoints are the Harbor Centre Observation Deck, located downtown at 555 West Hastings, and the 3,700-foot level of Grouse Mountain, reached by gondola car.

Vancouver is a city of parks and beaches, so it should come as no surprise that its pulse beats at Stanley Park. Surrounded on three sides by the sea, the park sprawls on the northwestern edge of downtown. Roads, trails and bicycle paths crisscross 1,000 acres of woods, meadows and beaches. The grounds offer views of downtown and the infamous Lion's Gate Bridge, which is far more beautiful to look at than to drive across.

Shopping, business and culture dominate downtown. Robsonstrasse, beginning at Robson and Burrard, offers a European atmosphere of boutiques, restaurants, delis and galleries. On rainy days, Pacific Centre, an underground mall along Georgia, makes an ideal excursion. Within shoppers' heaven, on the edge of Robson Square, stands the Vancouver Art Gallery: a genuine culture break for tired feet and spent pocketbooks.

Vancouver's likable Chinatown sprawls along Pender Street. But before reaching this lively neighborhood, Gastown – Vancouver's birthplace – calls out from its Water Street perch. It's definitely a "tourist trap," but for those who like cobbled streets and old buildings it's worth a side-trip. Then it's back to Pender for the exotic shops, markets and restaurants of Chinatown.

All trips to Vancouver must end at Granville Island, which is actually a peninsula butting out into False

Creek. Forget driving there. The smart traveler takes the cozy False Creek Ferry, which leaves the Vancouver Aquatic Center from within Sunset Beach Park. Granville Island boasts a mix of shops, restaurants and galleries and is home to the city's public market.

Travelers who love to play will find much to enjoy here. But those who take the time to discover the city will also find much to admire.

Travel Notes and Insider Tips

Interstate 5 becomes Provincial Highway 99, which leads downtown. Highway 7 and Trans-Canada 1 enter from the east. At the border, U.S. citizens may be asked to show proof of citizenship. Vancouver International Airport is a 30-minute drive from downtown.

Vancouver features many fine restaurants. Among the best are Cafe de Paris (a French bistro serving classic food – 687-1418), Le Gavroche (perhaps the city's best French restaurant – 685-3924), Corsi Trattoria (authentic Italian food – 987-9910), Caffe de Medici (another excellent Italian restaurant – 669-9322), The Teahouse at Stanley Park (good food with a view – 669-3281), Bandi's (Hungarian fare – 685-3391) and A Kettle of Fish (popular with locals – 682-6661). The hottest nightclubs in town are Richard on Richards (687-6794) and Pelican Bay in the Granville Island Hotel (683-7373). The area's most spectacular scenery and best outdoor adventures await at Capilano Suspension Bridge and Park (985-7474). In addition to the Vancouver Art Gallery (682-5621) and Stanley Park (681-1141), museum hoppers and park lovers should visit the Queen Elizabeth Arboretum and the Bloedel Conservatory (872-5513), University of British Columbia Museum of Anthropology (228-3825), Vancouver Maritime Museum (736-4431) and Vancouver Museum (736-4431). The city's best annual events are the Vancouver Sea Festival (669-4091) in mid-July and the Pacific National Exhibition (253-2311) in late August.

For more information about Vancouver, write or call: Greater Vancouver Convention & Visitors Bureau, #1625-1055 West Georgia Street, P.O. Box 11142, Royal Centre, Vancouver, B.C., Canada V6E 4C8 (682-2222). All of the above telephone numbers are in area code 604.

The Mandarin Vancouver

The Mandarin Vancouver is on a mission: It intends to climb to the top of the towering glass-and-steel mountain representing Vancouver's downtown hotels. If roots and breeding mean anything, the Mandarin already has a step up on its competition.

Operated by the Mandarin Oriental Hotel Group (MOHG), a Southeast Asian chain, this 197-room hotel welcomed its first guests on May 1, 1984. The opening marked the launching of a luxury flagship. Recognized by several magazines and travel writers as one of the world's best hotel chains, MOHG seeks to make its first North American hotel comparable to its Mandarin in Hong Kong – the Rolls-Royce of great hotels.

Like the world's finest automobile, the Mandarin Vancouver sports classic lines, touches of elegance and a host of extras. The Mandarin is geared toward the discriminating business person and the sophisticated leisure traveler. This approach translates into a first-class experience for all guests.

Upon arrival at the Howe Street entrance, doormen in tailcoats, top hats and white gloves usher visitors into the marbled lobby. Tasteful touches such as a hand-woven Taiping rug, an Italian custom-made chandelier and flower-filled marble planters add a subtle dignity to an environment completely convention-free and devoid of hurried activity.

Service, the testing ground for every luxury hotel, permeates the Mandarin. The pampering begins in the lobby with the smartly dressed and friendly mannered doormen, bellmen, concierge and reception staff, then flows through the floors in the form of efficient housekeepers, prompt room service and thoughtful amenities.

The third floor mirrors the hotel's attitude about service and sets the standards in Vancouver for guest facilities. Here travelers can employ a well-equipped business center – complete with secretarial services, a city-wide pager service, individual work desks, a reference library, telex, translation services, word processing, portable dictation equipment and a sitting room – then walk next door to a health club rivaling some of the city's best private spas. As well as a glass-enclosed pool and whirlpool, the club features squash and racquetball courts, an exercise room, changing rooms, saunas, color television, professional masseurs, qualified attendants, a juice bar and an exquisite billiards room.

Above the third floor rise the spacious guest rooms. Rich fabrics and handsome furnishings adorn each room. However, once again it is the extras which distinguish the Mandarin from other fine establishments: Bedside controls for television, radio and lighting; three telephones with international direct dial; completely stocked mini-bars; large writing desks; and Italian marbled bathrooms with separate baths and showers highlight the features. In addition, there are loads of perks, including oversized bath towels, terry robes, umbrellas in each closet, door chimes and morning newspaper delivery.

The hotel's cuisine equals its accommodations in quality. The gourmet restaurant, Cristal, features French fare. Entrees range from scallops of British Columbian salmon sautéed in calvados, to medallions of British Columbian pheasant stuffed with veal and fresh herbs.

With everything the Mandarin has to offer, even the superlatives carried in the stuffed bags of travel writers fall short in describing this hotel. It can safely be said, however, that the Mandarin is a first-class operation which does things right and is destined to hold a prominent position in a city rich with fine hotels.

Travel Notes and Insider Tips

Those entering the city via Trans-Canada 1 should exit west on Broadway. Take Broadway to Granville, turn north, cross the bridge and exit immediately onto Seymour. Follow Seymour to a left on Dunsmuir, then turn left onto Howe. Those coming in on Provincial 99 (which becomes Oak) should follow it to Broadway, then use the above directions. Vancouver International Airport is a 25-minute drive from the city's center.

The hotel is in the heart of Vancouver's shopping district. The best shopping is across the street in the underground mall, Pacific Centre, and nearby Robsonstrasse, Vancouver's chic European shopping experience. Art lovers should walk across Georgia to the Vancouver Art Gallery; park lovers must make the ten-minute drive to Stanley Park. Vancouver's information center is located in Robson Square, site of the gallery. See page 85 for more tips on Vancouver.

Only 17 of the Mandarin Vancouver's rooms are suites. Nevertheless, the standard rooms are spacious. Street noise is evident on the lower floors but not overwhelming. In addition to Cristal's, the hotel also features an informal restaurant, Le Café, a lounge, and a bar. Room doubles range from $190 to $205. Suites begin at $310. Reduced corporate rates and weekend rates are available. Cristal's entrees range from $17.75 to $22. All prices are Canadian, subject to change and provided only for comparison.

The Mandarin Vancouver
645 Howe Street
Vancouver, B.C., Canada V6C 2Y9
(604) 687-1122
(800) 663-0787 (Inside Canada)

Four Seasons Hotel

People the world over desire quality, and those who can afford it will settle for nothing less. For the hotel business this means providing consistently good service within first-class surroundings. Hotels which accomplish those goals grow and prosper; those which don't go the way of the dinosaur. The Four Seasons chain is a survivor.

Since 1961, when 30-year-old Isadore Sharp opened the Four Seasons Motor Hotel in Toronto, the company has been gaining in size and stature. Today Four Seasons operates 20 hotels, including Inn on the Park in London, The Ritz-Carlton in Chicago, The Pierre in New York and the Four Seasons Olympic in Seattle. Sharp's modest seed has flourished to become a garden of luxury.

In 1976, the Four Seasons Hotel in Vancouver opened. Located in the heart of downtown, it became one of Vancouver's finest hotels. For ten consecutive years AAA has recognized the hotel's level of excellence by presenting it with the club's Five Diamond Award. Not happy to rely on laurels, however, the hotel spent $5 million in 1985 renovating its accommodations and its public areas. For the traveler, the results translate into more space and a more elegant look.

The renovation reduced the hotel's number of rooms from 430 to 385. As a result, 45 new Deluxe Four Seasons Suites look out on the mountains as they climb above North Vancouver's high-rises and Burrard Inlet's gray waters.

Outside of the two split-level Penthouse Suites, these Four Seasons Suites represent the hotel's finest accommodations. French doors separate the bedrooms and living rooms, which are adorned with marbletop tables, overstuffed furniture, fresh flowers, two remote control televisions, telephones with two lines, and miniature bars. In the other guest rooms, renovation meant new beds, bedspreads, drapes, sheers and televisions. Public areas were also given a face lifting.

While refreshing and necessary, these improvements represent only cosmetic changes, though to the corporate traveler larger rooms mean more than just fresh make-up. Nevertheless, great hotels are like actors – handsome looks may open some doors, but excellent performances keep them from closing. Vancouver's Four Seasons Hotel knows how to put on a show.

The hotel's service ranks with the best: The front desk staff is amiable, the concierge is knowledgeable and accessible, room service is prompt, and housekeeping is efficient and unobtrusive. In addition, the list of amenities covers every need: 24-hour room service, 24-hour valet, valet parking, bathrobes in all guest rooms, complimentary shoeshine, twice-daily maid service, full concierge service, non-smoking floors, mini bars in all guest rooms, designer toiletries and hair-dryers in all bathrooms, and complimentary limousine service to downtown areas.

Just as its Seattle sister features that city's best function rooms and catering services, so does the Four Seasons Hotel in Vancouver. Its Park Ballroom accommodates 450 to 600 people, while ten other function rooms cater to groups of 40 to 180. Pleasantly unique, Le Pavillon, the hotel's gourmet banquet room, offers personalized menus for each client and a setting which combines royal Doulton china, Zwiesel crystal, antique silver, fresh flowers and friendly service.

There is little to fault here, which generally holds true for the entire Four Seasons chain. Perhaps, above all else, its willingness to maintain high standards, to try to stay atop an ever-expanding market, says it best when it comes to the Four Seasons.

Travel Notes and Insider Tips

From 99, cross the Granville Island Bridge and immediately exit onto Seymour. Follow this to a left on Dunsmuir, then turn left onto Howe. The hotel stands on the corner of Howe and Georgia Streets.

The Four Seasons Hotel rises above Pacific Centre, an underground mall with some 200 shops and restaurants. It sits across the street from the Vancouver Art Gallery and only a few blocks from Robsonstrasse. The hotel's fourth floor features an indoor/outdoor pool, sundeck, saunas, whirlpool, hot tub and exercise equipment. For more tips on Vancouver, see page 85.

Room doubles begin at $150. Four Seasons Suites start at $190. Penthouse Suites cost $780 and $950. Chartwell, the hotel's new fine dining restaurant, had not yet opened at this writing, so prices were not available. All prices are Canadian, subject to change and provided only for comparison.

Four Seasons Hotel
791 West Georgia Street
Vancouver, B.C., Canada V6C 2T4
(604) 689-9333
(800) 268-6282 (Reservations Only)

Wedgewood

Like its homonymic namesake, the Wedgewood Hotel stands for quality. Its owner, the preeminent Eleni Skalbania, would have it no other way.

Eleni is the driving force behind the Wedgewood's almost-overnight success in a competitive Vancouver market. This comes as no surprise to either her admirers or her detractors. Eleni Skalbania is the kind of person who makes things happen.

Eleni grew up in Greece, moved to Vancouver in 1960 and taught herself English, while studying accounting. She began developing a business career, which eventually included owning and operating the Georgia Hotel. In 1984, she purchased the Mayfair, a derelict hotel. Recognizing the rising popularity of elegant world-class small hotels, she determined that her acquisition would be molded into just such a place.

Eleni poured $7.5 million into her dream (which includes the $4.5 million purchase price). The building's insides were gutted and rebuilt; the 13-story structure received several coats of fresh paint. Eleni personally supervised all the construction and was responsible for the interior decorating. Her personal collections of antiques and works of art were moved from her home to the hotel to accent the public areas. While nails were being set and carpeting laid, Eleni called the hotel home.

On June 7, 1984, the Wedgewood hosted its first guests. Marble, brass and polished woods welcomed an upscale clientele – mostly young, professional and affluent. Success was immediate. In its first three months, the Wedgewood experienced occupancy rates between 65 and 75 percent.

Today the 94-room hotel continues its rise toward the top. Behind the palladian windows of the Bacchus Bistro, lunch and dinner crowds vie for tables within its garden setting. The French Nouvelle cuisine and the elegant decor of skylights and an ornate fireplace draw discriminating diners to sup in The Wedgewood Room. And the intimate air of the guest rooms – enhanced by pastels, potted palms and satiny comforters – lure both the corporate and leisure traveler.

Any hotel can offer antiques, fancy trim and elegant ambiance. In fact, many do. Nevertheless, the Wedgewood stands out from the crowd.

Again, the reason seems to be Eleni Skalbania. She puts in 18-hour days, waltzing about the hotel greeting her guests and seeing to it that they're receiving first-class service. Little things are important to her. For instance, the hotel could purchase perfectly good bakery products, but it doesn't. All the baked goods are prepared in the hotel's kitchen. Guest histories are maintained on every client, so special needs can be anticipated. And rumor has it that Eleni once went so far as to personally press the shirt of a harried guest.

Other amenities and special services also make their mark here. There are photocopying and secretarial services; a baby sitting service; mini-bars, remote con-

trol televisions and teleconferencing-capable phones in all rooms; fireplaces adorning some one-bedroom suites; complimentary shoeshine; 24-hour room service; complimentary continental breakfast; morning newspaper delivery; and valet parking.

Small hotels such as the Wedgewood offer travelers an elegant alternative to the giants in the industry. Everyone benefits by their existence.

Travel Notes and Insider Tips

The Wedgewood stands in the heart of downtown, across the street from Robson Square. From 99, cross the Granville Island Bridge and immediately exit onto Seymour. Take Seymour to Georgia, turn left, then take another left onto Hornby to the hotel.

One-third of the rooms here are suites; they represent first-class bargains. Reservations should be made three to four weeks in advance. See page 85 for tips on Vancouver.

Double rates range from $110 to $160 for standards, and $175 to $225 for suites. Dinner entrees in The Wedgewood Room run from $15.95 to $23.95. All prices are Canadian, subject to change and provided for comparison only.

Wedgewood
845 Hornby Street
Vancouver, B.C., Canada V6Z 1V1
(604) 689-7777
(800) 663-0666

The Granville Island Hotel

Beautiful people everywhere! The boardwalk sways with long flowered skirts and blushes with skimpy tops. Bronzed bodies call attention to sailing yachts moored restlessly in the marina. The lunch crowd sips designer water and caresses imported beer. Waiters smile from behind dark sunglasses and saunter about.

While Granville Island floats a great distance from places such as Rio, the scene here, especially at the hotel, mirrors the carefree attitudes which dominate the world's holiday places – life is beautiful and so are the people.

Fun! That's what The Granville Island Hotel sells, and it does it very well. In the great glass atrium that divides the hotel in two, the Cyrus P. Windless Kite Flying Machine watches from its lofty perch. Below, the trendy in-crowd begins gathering at 7 p.m. for a night of urban theater. Pelican Bay, the hotel's chic disco, is one of Vancouver's hottest nightspots and lures pleasure seekers by the boutique-full.

Upstairs, guests fortunate enough to occupy a room somewhere other than above the club, lounge about their California-style accommodations. Mirrors, cedar, shutters and vaulted ceilings dominate their surroundings. Before descending for an evening of dining and

dancing, some climb to the rooftop for a dip in the glass-enclosed Jacuzzi. It represents a ritual which prepares the mind and the spirit for a night of expectations.

Breakfast is often a late affair, followed by a tour of the Island (which is really an isthmus). Revival marks this hodgepodge of industrial buildings which rise above the waters of False Creek and hover below the Granville Island Bridge.

The hum of yesterday's industry has faded into the past. Today the sounds of tourists echo in and around the clusters of corrugated steel. Restaurants, shops and galleries now call these warehouses home, while the Granville Island Public Market bustles as the center of commercial activity.

Despite the busy streets by day, crowded with shoppers and sightseers, the hotel remains the Island's focal point for the affluent hip. It's a symbol of the Island's revitalization and its devotion to gaiety.

Travel Notes and Insider Tips

From the south, follow 99, which becomes Oak Street, to 6th Avenue. Turn left and follow the signs to Granville Island.

Obviously, this hotel isn't for everyone. If you're looking for a quiet environment, it's best to choose another location. However, Granville Island does feature views, water and excellent shopping, not to mention the party atmosphere. The hotel's marina has facilities for 50 boats and offers connections to the hotel's satellite television system, as well as its telephone, power and water lines. Expect summer crowds. It's always best to make reservations for dining, whether they're for the hotel or one of the nearby restaurants. See page 85 for tips on Vancouver.

Room rates range from $125 to $375 for a double. Ask for a room away from the disco. Some of the rooms have balconies and many offer good views. Food at the bistro and the restaurant is moderately priced. All prices are Canadian, subject to change and provided only for comparison.

The Granville Island Hotel
1253 Johnston Street
Granville Island
Vancouver, B.C., Canada V6H 3R9
(604) 683-7373

Park Royal Hotel

Sometimes even the most enthusiastic city traveler requires a break from the pace of downtown. Yet knowing they must be close to the city's pulse, they seek a hotel not far from the crowds. Greater Vancouver features one of the best. Located across the Lion's Gate Bridge in West Vancouver, the Park Royal Hotel boasts a reputation for both fine dining and pleasant surroundings.

The two-story Tudor-style hotel rambles alongside a manicured lawn, where tulips and azaleas bloom and guests sip wine while enjoying their terrace perch. At the edge of the grounds, trees line the Capilano River, which washes over giant boulders on its way to join the sea.

Inside the hotel, Mario Corsi, manager extraodinaire, greets guests with genuine friendliness. "It's important that my guests know I care about them," Mario says. "People like the real things in life. They are looking for warmth and personal service. That's what we want to give them."

Mario's easy style has helped to make the Park Royal a popular and prosperous hotel. Not only do the 30 rooms enjoy a 90 percent occupancy rate, but the hotel's restaurant – the Tudor Room – draws connoisseurs of fine food from throughout Greater Vancouver. Good reasons exist for this. The rooms feature a residential comfort, while the restaurant boasts excellent food.

Belgian drapes, country pine antiques and overstuffed furniture enhance amenities such as remote control televisions and whirlpool baths. The guest rooms welcome good books and inspire conversation. Rooms, especially those with river views, are hard to leave.

However, as the sun begins to fade and the smells of Chateaubriand and Bombay curried shrimp start wafting down the hallways, books are laid aside, conversations cease and feet beat a path to the Tudor Room.

Nothing but the freshest of foods grace the restaurant's china. While wood paneling and heavy beams mirror an English inn, forget Yorkshire pudding. The emphasis here is on locally grown Northwest products. Both the restaurant's ambiance and its cuisine approach excellence. In fact, the Tudor Room has earned the Mobil Guide's prestigious Four Star Award.

Following dinner the downstairs pub lures many diners to top their evenings with a few piano tunes and several nightcaps. A mix of people, low lights and friendly service promote warmth in a fashion typical of the hotel.

Although the Park Royal sits in the suburbs, it is only ten minutes from downtown. Vancouver's pulse may not be felt here, but it is never far away. And while the beat rushes on in the city's heart, it just eases itself along at the Park Royal Hotel.

Travel Notes and Insider Tips

From Vancouver, cross the Lion's Gate Bridge, then exit onto Marine Drive. Travel west into West Vancouver, turn right onto Taylor Way, then right again on Clyde.

Shoppers will find that the nearby Park Royal Shopping Centre meets their mall needs, while the shops of downtown Vancouver sit only a short drive away. If visitors don't wish to drive downtown, Vancouver's Sea-Bus bridges North Vancouver and the city. A path alongside the Capilano River makes an excellent walk: South leads to Ambleside Park, which fronts the narrows; north travels into the hills. The following is a must: Drive up Capilano Road to the Capilano suspension bridge, Capilano Canyon, Capilano Lake and the Grouse Mountain skyride. Travelers will never forget these views. See page 85 for more tips on Vancouver.

Room doubles range from $76 to $140. Odd-numbered rooms 205 through 217 offer the most privacy and the best views. Dinner entrees range from $10.95 to $19.75. All prices are Canadian, subject to change and provided only for comparison.

Park Royal Hotel
440 Clyde Avenue
West Vancouver, B.C., Canada V7T 2J7
(604) 926-5511

Hastings House

The Gulf Islands spread their fingers between British Columbia's lower mainland and Vancouver Island's southeast side. They extend north from the San Juan Islands, actually making up part of that same archipelago. However, international politics long ago assured that these two chains would never be more than distant cousins.

Located just north of Vancouver Island's thumb, a short ferry ride from Sydney, sprawls Saltspring Island. Measuring seven miles across and 20 miles long, it represents the largest piece of real estate in the Gulf Islands. Some 6,000 people, many of them artisans, inhabit Saltspring's forested hills and patches of farmland.

Protected by a moderate climate, residents pursue a low-key lifestyle here. High-rises, condos, department stores and highways simply don't exist; pottery, painting, weaving, farming, fishing and beachcombing do. In itself, this tranquil setting may not be enough to lure travelers, which is just fine with the residents. However, perched on a rise overlooking the quaint harbor town of Ganges sits a hideaway which seduces visitors from throughout North America. For those who can afford it, this resort spells paradise.

Hastings House, a 25-acre country estate, ranks as one of the world's best small resorts. Pristine surroundings, elegant accommodations, gourmet food and impeccable service represent a way of life here. That means rates which dig deep into pocketbooks. But for travelers who value pampering and relish excellence, the cost is worth it.

Pebbled paths meander about manicured lawns lush with fruit trees, tall evergreens and flower beds. A large vegetable garden draws the attention of chickens and ducks – grazing sheep seem not to notice. Salt air and the echoes of blocks ringing against spars rise from the harbor below, bathing the grounds in island tranquillity. Four stuccoed and half-timbered buildings dot the landscape.

The Manor House is the focal point of the estate. Upstairs, a library nook separates two suites which look out to sea. Open beams, hardwood floors and stone fireplaces accent the plush surroundings, while downstairs, the dining room awaits.

Every meal at the Hastings House resembles an exclusive dinner party. Before the five-course repast is served, guests gather around the cowled stone fireplace to sip sherry and engage in conversation. Casement windows, handsome antiques, plank floors and Persian carpets lend an air of aristocracy. At dinnertime, each guest or couple is escorted to separate tables, where they are presented with hand-lettered personalized menus. The fare is set, but the same entrees are never featured more than once a month. Both the food and the service are excellent.

The accommodations in the outlying buildings offer the same luxury which dominates the Manor House. Distinctive decor, service and ambiance mark each room or suite.

Adjacent to the Manor House stands the resort's creme de la creme – the Farmhouse. It contains two spacious parlor suites. Each features two bathrooms, a brick fireplace, front and back porches, an upstairs bedroom, a downstairs living room and a wet bar. Wedgwood cups and saucers stand ready for tea, while cream stays fresh in the refrigerator.

Nearby Post Cottage presents a portrait of an English summer home, with wicker furniture, green and yellow fabrics, a wood stove, and French doors which open onto

the lawn. Behind the cottage rests the Barn, featuring two parlor suites and two guest rooms. The tenth accommodation is the cozy Snug, which hides under the restaurant.

Eiderdown quilts, thick bath towels, personalized door plaques, private telephones, fresh flowers, bed turndowns and complimentary continental breakfasts, which are quietly delivered to guest rooms promptly at 7, make Hastings House a resort which is expensive but very special.

Travel Notes and Insider Tips

Saltspring Island can be reached by B.C. Ferry (604-669-1211) from either Tsawwassen on the mainland or Swartz Bay on Vancouver Island. Advance reservations are recommended June through August. Charter planes also serve Saltspring.

Hastings House serves readers, writers and dreamers best. But the island does offer some interesting features. On Saturday mornings, for instance, Ganges hosts a farmers' market, which offers visitors an opportunity to meet some of the locals and to sample some of their fresh produce. Sometimes known as The Crafty Island, several unique shops and galleries dot the area: Visit Art Craft, an island co-operative, across from the Ganges Marina, The Loom Room in Mouat's Mall, and Ewart Gallery on Saltspring Way. Beachcombing here is good – fishing is better. Halibut, sole, smelt, salmon, steelhead and cutthroat abound. The island's best viewpoint is atop Maxwell Mountain by way of Cranberry Road.

During July and August, Hastings House reqires minimum stays of two nights on weekends. The resort does not accept reservations for children under 16. All accommodations feature large private bathrooms and either fireplaces or wood stoves. Daily rates range from $150 to $240. The five-course dinner costs $34 per person (well worth the price). Meeting, seminar and corporate rates are available. All prices are Canadian, subject to change and provided only for comparison.

Hastings House
Box 1110
Ganges, B.C., Canada V0S 1E0
(604) 537-2362
(800) 661-1345 (Western Canada)

Whistler

For two decades skiers have flocked to Whistler and, since 1980, Blackcomb Mountains. Together their powdery slopes offer some of the finest skiing in North America. Yet Whistler is much more than a skier's paradise.

Calling Whistler a resort is a little like calling Badrutt's Palace Hotel in St. Moritz a country inn. Actually, the word Whistler refers to both a mountain and a nine-mile-long valley that in 1975 became Canada's first and only resort municipality. Today Whistler boasts two mountains, dozens of inns and lodges, and a central village that mirrors the quintessential community of the '80s.

The village is a colony of hotels, condominiums, lodges, restaurants, lounges, specialty shops and basic services. In the background, snow-clad Blackcomb rises above multi-gabled roofs – smoke curls from their armies of chimney stacks. In the square, children, singles, parents and grandparents crisscross the cobbled courtyards. Many shoulder skis and rock forth in their colorful ski boots. The village's excited pulse marks a new era in Whistler's history.

"We're finally coming of age," Drew Meredith, president of the Whistler Resort Association, says. "Word of mouth is causing volume to grow. The village spearheaded the growth. Before 1980 there were a couple of gas stations, a few small grocery stores, a couple of rustic hotels and the best skiing in North America. Now we have elegant accommodations and fine restaurants to go with that skiing."

In total there are some 30 fine hotels and condominium-style facilities (nearly 20 of them are located in the village) represented by the Association. In addition, there are a number of smaller lodges and guest houses available outside of the perimeters of the Association. The valley also boasts 16 restaurants and a variety of nightspots.

A typical condo suite, such as the one found in the 22-room Carleton Lodge, features wall-to-wall carpeting, modern furnishings, a fireplace and a completely stocked kitchen. Restaurants offer cuisine from continental at Araxi's to Italian at Umberto's.

Skiing season, including cross-country and helo-skiing, runs from late November to early May. It still represents Whistler's main attraction. However, from April to November, warm-weather visitors discover a medley of leisure activities as well: golf on the 18-hole, par-72 Arnold Palmer championship course; canoeing on one of Whistler's lakes or the River of Golden Dreams; trout fishing on Alta, Nita, Alpha, Lost, Green, Cheakamus and Rainbow lakes; horseback riding or mountain hiking; river rafting and wind surfing; and just plain old sightseeing.

It is clear that Whistler has become a resort for all seasons. There is little doubt that once the word gets out, Whistler will begin drawing travelers in large numbers year-round.

Travel Notes and Insider Tips

From Vancouver, take Highway 99 to Whistler (about a 90-minute drive). From Seattle, take I-5 to the Canadian border, then Exit 275 to Highway 15. Drive through Cloverdale to Trans-Canada 1 west, which accesses Highway 99. Major airlines serve Vancouver International Airport, where rental cars are available. In addition, Maverick Coach Lines (604-255-1171) provides daily bus transportation from Vancouver to Whistler, as does British Columbia Rail (604-984-5246).

Dress here is mostly casual and athletic, but singles may wish to impress. Good advice is to come prepared for all occasions, including the possibility of inclement weather.

Room rates and dining costs vary greatly at Whistler. Holidays and winter weekends should be booked several months ahead, while other times three to six weeks in advance are appropriate.

Whistler
Whistler Resort Association
P.O. Box 1400
Whistler, B.C., Canada V0N 1B0
(604) 932-4222
(604) 222-2554 (In Vancouver)
(206) 467-7554 (In Seattle)

Little Gun Lake Lodge

Mountain magic blankets the area. Rising in every direction, British Columbia's Chilcotin Range casts rugged looks at the sprawling valley below. This is the middle of "Nowhere," and "Nowhere" is where all of nature wraps itself in magnificent splendor. It is also the home of Little Gun Lake Lodge.

Located six hours northeast of Vancouver, the log lodge sits on the shores of Little Gun Lake. The Coast Mountains look down on its steep silvery roof. Entering the lake on its western shore, Penrose Creek plays a nonstop melody. Bees buzz about the rocky beaches; dragonflies flit about the reeds. Ducks cruise across the still waters, trailing V-shaped wakes. Rainbow trout leap into the air, then splash back into their dark sanctuary. Birches, cottonwoods and firs form a ring of green. The air smells of nothing but air.

Inside the lodge, massive logs rise great heights before meeting a canted ceiling. A fire crackles within a granite fireplace, while the sun cascades through paned windows, sending shards of gold across green leather sofas and overstuffed chairs. Alongside shelves of books, a door leads to the main floor guest rooms; in the opposite corner, stairs wind to three more accommodations which dot the mezzanine level.

Glass doors lead into the L-shaped dining room, which overlooks a tiny pier as it juts out into the lake. Oriental carpets, hanging plants, natural woods and gentle wallpaper lend an air of comfort. The food is gourmet; the wine list is excellent.

On the lawns outside sit a recreation building and two private cabins. Exercise equipment, a ping pong table and a whirlpool occupy one; escape resides in the others.

Emerson may have been right when he proclaimed, "Nothing can bring you peace but yourself." But then again, Emerson never knew of Little Gun Lake Lodge.

Travel Notes and Insider Tips

Without its isolation, Little Gun Lake Lodge would lose much of its magic: It might also be easier to reach. Drivers can expect glorious scenery, from lush forests to majestic mountains to deep canyons. They can also expect about 60 miles of winding, sometimes narrow, gravel road. The best way (but not the most scenic) is to take Trans-Canada Highway 1 east and north to Lytton, then Provincial 12 to Lillooet. From there, take gravel Highway 40 to Gold Bridge and keep repeating, "This is worth it! This is worth it!" Non-driving alternatives also exist: British Columbia Rail from North Vancouver to Lillooet, where guests are met by the lodge's innkeepers, or float plane from either Vancouver or Squamish via Squamish Air Service (604-689-1911) or from Seattle by Lake Union Air (206-284-2784).

This is gold mining country and the ruins of several mines wither nearby. Don't miss driving to both the Bralorne Mine and Pioneer Mine. Before leaving Bralorne, visit the Bralorne Pioneer Store, which carries everything from gourmet food to local lore. In Gold Bridge, a town of about 100, stop at the hotel for a cold drink: The entire place is a tribute to the past. Gold Bridge is the area's only real town, which emphasizes the remoteness of this region. Besides sightseeing, outdoor activities include fishing (license required, which can be purchased locally), boating (rowboats, a canoe and a sailboat are available at no charge), swimming in Little Gun Lake, hiking, mountain climbing, gold panning, horseback riding and bird watching.

The lodge is only open from early May to late October. Room number one features a fireplace and a large private bath ($76/night). Rooms two and three are roomy with private baths ($68/night). Room six has a balcony and a shower ($60/night). Rooms four and five have balconies and share a hall shower ($56/night). The cabins have sun decks and private baths ($60/night). Two meal plans are available: Full pension – three meals daily – is $33 a day per adult; children under 12 pay $22 a day. In addition, guests may order individual meals. Special packages are also available. All prices are Canadian, subject to change and provided only for comparison.

Little Gun Lake Lodge
General Delivery
Gold Bridge, B.C., Canada V0K 1P0
(604) 238-2277

Northern California

SAN FRANCISCO

THE STANFORD COURT
Nob Hill
905 California Street
San Francisco, CA 94108
(415) 989-3500
(800) 622-0957 (Inside California)
(800) 227-4736 (Inside United States)

Located on Nob Hill and considered to be San Francisco's best hotel. Winner of the Mobil Five Star and the Diplôme de l'Excellence Éuropéene awards. Not a convention hotel. Exceptional dining in Fournou's Ovens. Four-hundred-two rooms and suites. Rooms start at $135; suites run from $330.

THE FAIRMONT HOTEL
Nob Hill
950 Mason Avenue
San Francisco, CA 94106
(415) 772-5000
(800) 527-4727

Located atop Nob Hill, four blocks from Union Square and the financial district. Very posh. Seven-hundred rooms and elegant public spaces. Winner of the Mobil Four Star and AAA Five Diamond awards. Seven gourmet restaurants and the Venetian Room supper club. Suites range from $425 to $3,500.

The Fairmont Hotel

THE PACIFIC PLAZA
501 Post Street
San Francisco, CA 94102
(415) 441-7100
(800) 792-9837 (Inside California)
(800) 227-3184 (Inside United States)

Located downtown just one block from Union Square. An elegant small hotel with 122 guest rooms. The Donatello serves excellent northern Italian cuisine. Rooms run from $135; suites start at $275.

STANYAN PARK HOTEL
750 Stanyan Street
San Francisco, CA 94117
(415) 751-1000

Located on the edge of Golden Gate Park. It was built in 1904 and recently restored. Decor is Queen Anne Victorian. Thirty-six rooms. Rates range from $55 to $145.

THE HUNTINGTON HOTEL
1075 California Street
San Francisco, CA 94108
(415) 474-5400
(800) 652-1539 (Inside California)
(800) 227-4683 (Inside United States)

This is an elegant 143-room hotel atop Nob Hill overlooking Huntington Park. Its guests often include heads of state, European nobility, opera stars and other celebrities. Each room and suite is individually decorated; most have wet bars. The hotel's 1962 Silver Cloud II Rolls-Royce is available to transport guests downtown for shopping or business. Doubles range from $135 to $545.

Huntington Hotel

Meadowood

MEADOWOOD
900 Meadowood Lane
St. Helena, CA 94574
(707) 963-3646
(800) 458-8080 (Inside California)

An exclusive resort located on 256 acres in the heart of the Napa Valley. Country club atmosphere. Nine-hole golf course. Tennis courts. Swimming pool. California country cuisine in the restaurant. Executive conference center. Sixty luxury accommodations ranging in price from $115 to $650.

AUBERGE DU SOLEIL
180 Rutherford Hill Road
Rutherford, CA 94573
(707) 963-1211

Set on a hillside overlooking the Napa Valley. Offers the ambiance of a French country inn. Swimming pool. Tennis courts. Outstanding dining features a combination of French Nouvelle and California-style cuisine. Thirty-six rooms and suites ranging from $180 to $420.

HARVEST INN
One Main Street
St. Helena, CA 94574
(707) 963-9463

Located in the heart of the Napa Valley on a 21-acre working vineyard. English Tudor-style accommodations. Swimming pool. Jacuzzi. Thirty-two rooms – most have brick fireplaces. Rates range from $85 to $310.

MOUNT VIEW HOTEL
1457 Lincoln Avenue
Calistoga, CA 94515
(707) 942-6877

Located in the Napa Valley, 75 miles north of San Francisco. Art Deco decor and architecture. Spa treatments available. Swimming pool. Jacuzzi. Good American food. Thirty-four rooms and suites, ranging in price from $45 to $125.

SILVERADO
1600 Atlas Peak Road
Napa, CA 94558
(707) 257-0200

Located 50 miles northeast of San Francisco in the heart of the wine country. Clusters of condominium units surround an antebellum mansion. Two 18-hole golf courses. Eight swimming pools. The largest tennis complex in Northern California. Two-hundred-sixty-nine units, ranging in price from $145 to $335.

SONOMA MISSION INN AND SPA
P.O. Box I
Boyes Hot Springs, CA 95416
(707) 996-1041
(800) 862-4945 (Inside California)
(800) 358-9022 (Inside United States)

An elegant inn and fitness resort located 40 miles north of San Francisco. The 97-room California mission-style building was constructed in 1927 and renovated in 1980. The European-style spa opened in 1981. Room rates range from $110 to $375.

Sonoma Mission Inn and Spa

The Wine Country Inn

THE WINE COUNTRY INN
1152 Lodi Lane
St. Helena, CA 94574
(707) 963-7077

Perched on a knoll overlooking Napa Valley vineyards. Built in 1975 but boasting a historic look. Swimming pool. Spa. Twenty-five rooms with private bathrooms. Rates range from $85 to $145.

MARIN COUNTY

CASA MADRONA HOTEL
801 Bridgeway
Sausalito, CA 94965
(415) 332-0502

Located on a hill overlooking Sausalito, just ten minutes north of the Golden Gate Bridge. A romantic and elegant hotel. Wonderful views of the bay. French Nouvelle and California cuisine served in the restaurant. Twenty-nine rooms and three cottages, ranging in price from $60 to $275.

Casa Madrona Hotel

NORTH COAST

HILL HOUSE INN
P.O. Box 625
Mendocino, CA 95460
(707) 937-0554

A New England-style inn offering ocean views. Décor is a combination of Victorian and modern. Peaceful surroundings. All 44 guest rooms feature private baths. The accommodations range in price from $65 to $110.

THE GINGERBREAD MANSION
400 Berding Street
Ferndale, CA 95536
(707) 786-4000

A magnificent Victorian mansion set in the historic community of Ferndale, 260 miles north of San Francisco. Eight guest rooms – five with private baths. Afternoon tea. Complimentary home-cooked breakfast. Personalized attention. Rates range from $55 to $85.

All prices in this section are for single or double occupancy and indicate only a range of in-season rates. They are subject to change and are provided only for comparison.

Photographs in this section were provided by these hostelries.

The Best of the Rest

OREGON

Bar M Ranch
Route 1
Adams, OR 97810
(503) 566-3381

Located 31 miles east of Pendleton in the Blue Mountains. Excellent hospitality. Horseback riding. Fishing. Simple accommodations. Good family-style food.

House on the Hill
P.O. Box 187
Oceanside, OR 97134
(503) 842-6030

Marvelous oceanside location atop Maxwell Point. Overlooks Three Arch Rocks and Oceanside. Cracker-box accommodations. No food.

The Inn at Otter Crest
P.O. Box 50
Otter Rock, OR 97369
(503) 765-2111
(800) 452-2101 (Inside Oregon)
(800) 547-2181 (Outside Oregon)

First-class resort on the Oregon Coast. Two-hundred-fifty deluxe rooms and suites. Splendid views and surroundings. Swimming pool. Tennis. Sauna. Jacuzzi.

Ireland's Rustic Lodges
P.O. Box 774
Gold Beach, OR 97444
(503) 247-7718

Good location on the southern Oregon Coast, within driving distance of Redwood National Park. Good beaches. Fishing. Jet-boat trips. Cottage accommodations.

Kah-Nee-Ta
P.O. Box K
Warm Springs, OR 97761
(503) 553-1112
(800) 452-1138 (Inside Oregon)
(800) 547-1102 (Western States)

A posh resort located in the Warm Springs Indian Reservation. Modern lodge. Cottages. Teepees. Mineral bath. Swimming pool. Horseback riding. Golf. Tennis. Stark environment of Central Oregon.

Lake Creek Lodge
Sisters, OR 97759
(503) 595-6331

Located about ten miles west of Sisters in the Oregon Cascades. Family resort. Cottages. Perched alongside a pond. Recreational opportunities abound. Isolated.

Mark Antony Hotel
212 East Main Street
P.O. Box 1240
Ashland, OR 97520
(503) 482-1721
(800) 544-5448

A restored historic hotel built in the 1920s. Art Deco style. Eighty-two rooms. Antiques. Restaurant and lounge. Swimming pool.

Metolius River Lodges
P.O. Box 110
Camp Sherman, OR 97730
(503) 595-6290

Located in the Oregon Cascades, 38 miles northwest of Bend. Surrounded by mountain forests. Fishing. Downhill and cross-country skiing. Fully equipped cabins.

Mount Bachelor Village
19717 Mount Bachelor Drive
Bend, OR 97702
(503) 389-5900
(800) 452-9846 (Inside Oregon)
(800) 547-5204 (Outside Oregon)

Modern condominium resort located 18 miles from Mt. Bachelor. Swimming pool. Serious tennis village in summer; ski resort in winter.

Paradise Ranch Inn
7000-D Monument Drive
Grants Pass, OR 97526
(503) 479-4333

A first-class resort located north of Grants Pass in the Rogue River Valley. Luxury surroundings. Horseback riding. Fishing. Golf. Tennis. Excellent dining.

Rock Springs Guest Ranch
64201 Tyler Road
Bend, OR 97701
(503) 382-1957

Located ten miles northwest of Bend. Family vacations. Horseback riding. Tennis. Volleyball. Swimming pool. Fly fishing. Cabins.

Spindrift Bed & Breakfast
2990 Beach Loop Road
Bandon, OR 97411
(503) 347-2275

Perched on a bluff 50 feet above the beach, this home features open vistas of the ocean and the hospitality of people who care. Home-cooked breakfasts. Two guest rooms. Excellent beachcombing and storm watching.

Steamboat Inn
HC 60, Box 36
Idleyld Park, OR 97447
(503) 496-3495
(503) 498-2411

A small resort on the banks of the North Umpqua River in southern Oregon. Rustic cabins. Excellent fishing. Superb food.

Timberline Lodge
Government Camp, OR 97028
(503) 231-5400
(800) 452-1335 (Inside Oregon)
(800) 547-1406 (Western States)

Built in 1937 of stone and hand-hewn timbers. Recently restored. Spectacular setting within the Mount Hood National Forest. Skiing. Hiking. Heated Pool. Sauna.

WASHINGTON

The Breakers
P.O. Box 428
Long Beach, WA 98631
(206) 642-2727

Seventy-two condominium units sitting alongside the beach on the Long Beach Peninsula. Modest decor. Swimming pool. Spa.

The Captain Whidbey
Route 1, Box 32
Coupeville, WA 98239
(206) 678-4097

A log inn built in 1907 overlooking Penn Cove. Historic setting. Lodging is simple. It is a mixed bag of inn rooms, cabins and motel-like units. Good food and hospitality.

Crescent Bar Resort
Quincy, WA 98848
(509) 787-1511

A condominium-style resort located 24 miles south of Wenatchee and 30 miles southeast of Mission Ridge ski area. Sits on an island in the Columbia River, surrounded by basalt cliffs. Swimming pool. Beaches. Golf. Tennis. Marina.

Hidden Valley Ranch
Route 2, Box 111
Cle Elum, WA 98922
(509) 674-2422

A working horse ranch on a meadowland southwest of Blewett Pass. Rustic cabins. Family-style meals. Horseback riding. Eastern Washington sunshine.

Lonesome Cove Resort
5810-A Lonesome Cove Road
Friday Harbor, WA 98250
(206) 378-4477

Five log cabins along the beach of Spieden Channel. Located near Roche Harbor on San Juan Island within pristine surroundings. Fireplaces. Decks. Library. Fishing. Great views. No televisions. Peaceful.

The Sandpiper Beach Resort
P.O. Box A
Pacific Beach, WA 98571
(206) 276-4580

Two wooden buildings containing apartments. Nestled in a wooded environment on the edge of the beach. Kite flying. Beachcombing. Clamming. Views. Peaceful. Winter storm watching.

The Resort Semiahmoo
5660 Drayton Harbor Road
Blaine, WA 98230
(206) 332-8588

A new posh resort located on a spit just south of the Canadian border. Two-hundred-room inn. Conference center. Athletic club. Golf. Tennis. Swimming pools. Marina. Fishing. Boating.

Sun Mountain Lodge
P.O. Box 1000
Winthrop, WA 98862
(509) 996-2211
(800) 572-0493 (Inside Washington)

Nestled in the wilderness, 1,500 feet above the Methow Valley. Magnificent views of the North Cascade Mountains. Swimming pool. Tennis. Hiking. Horseback riding. Skiing.

BRITISH COLUMBIA

Aguilar House Resort
Bamfield, B.C., Canada V0R 1B0
(604) 728-3323

Located in a tiny fishing village on the west coast of Vancouver Island. Remote. Peaceful. Small lodge and three cottages. Fishing. Hiking. Beachcombing. Boating. Open April to October.

April Point
P.O. Box One
Campbell River, B.C., Canada V9W 4Z9
(604) 285-3329

A top fishing lodge on Vancouver Island. Friendly hospitality. Good food. Pristine surroundings. Open April to October.

Lake Okanagan Resort
P.O. Box 1321
Station A
Kelowna, B.C., Canada V1Y 7V8
(604) 769-3511

Located on the shores of Lake Okanagan in the midst of fruit orchards and vineyards. Condominiums. Chalets. Hotel suites or studios. Swimming pools. Jacuzzis. Saunas. Tennis. Golf. Horseback riding. Water sports. Marina.

Laurel Point Inn
680 Montreal Street
Victoria, B.C., Canada V8V 1Z8
(604) 386-8721

Victoria's best contemporary hotel. Overlooks the inner harbor. One-hundred-thirty spacious rooms. Tennis. Swimming pool. Whirlpool. Saunas. Excellent service. Fine dining. Conveniently located to downtown.

Sandy Beach Lodge
P.O. Box 8
Naramata, B.C., Canada V0H 1N0
(604) 496-5765

A log lodge and cabins situated on the beach alongside Lake Okanagan. Tennis. Swimming pool. Family vacations. One of B.C.'s most popular resorts.

Sundance Guest Ranch
P.O. Box 489
Ashcroft, B.C., Canada V0K 1A0
(604) 453-2422
(604) 453-2554

A working ranch in the midst of British Columbia's high country. Horseback riding. Swimming pool. Excellent food. Good accommodations.

The Westin Bayshore
1601 West Georgia Street
Vancouver, B.C., Canada V6G 2V4
(604) 682-3377

Features the most scenic location of Vancouver's downtown hotels. Looks out on the harbor, Stanley Park and the mountains. Five-hundred-twenty rooms. Health club. Yacht charters. Spotty service.

Index to Towns and Cities